Taken on March 20, 1943, this photograph shows F6F-3 Hellcat fighters with their wings folded and SBD-4 Dauntless dive bombers on the flight deck of USS ESSEX, CV-9, during the carrier's shakedown cruise. At this time, the aircraft were painted in the Blue-Gray over Light Gray scheme. (National Archives)

U. S. NAVY AND MARINE
CARRIER BASED AIRCRAFT
OF WORLD WAR II

by Bert Kinzey
and Rock Roszak

TABLE OF CONTENTS

Rear Cover: This two-view drawing illustrates the TBD-1 Devastator, crewed by ARM2c W. D. (Don) Horton, in the colorful pre-war scheme used by the United States Navy. The overall aircraft was painted with an aluminum lacquer, and the upper wings were Chrome Yellow. BuNo. 0323 featured a True Blue tail used by all squadrons assigned to USS ENTERPRISE, CV-6. The aircraft was assigned to the squadron's first section, signified by the Insignia Red colors on the cowling and the stripes on the upper wing. The nose color was only applied to the upper cowling, signifying that the airplane was the second aircraft assigned to the section. (Artwork by Rock Roszak)

CONTRIBUTORS AND SOURCES

Lloyd Jones	John Shoulders	Warren Munkasy	Grumman Aerospace
Vought Aircraft	Eastern Aircraft	U. S. Navy	U. S. Marine Corps
National Naval Aviation Museum	National Archives	U. S. Marine Corps Aviation Museum	

The authors express a special word of thanks to Hill Goodspeed at the National Naval Aviation Museum for his help during the research of this book. Appreciation is also expressed to Bill Johnson at the museum for arranging for detailed photography of some of the aircraft types that appear in this book. Detail & Scale highly recommends this museum, located at NAS Pensacola, Florida, and encourage everyone to visit and support this outstanding facility. Thanks are also expressed to Mike Starn at the U. S. Marine Corps Museum of Aviation at Quantico, Virginia. Mr. Starn arranged for the author to take detailed photographs of the museum's rare F4F-4 Wildcat. Detail & Scale also highly recommends this museum and we encourage aviation enthusiasts to visit and support this fine facility.

ISBN: 978-1-9829621-2-8

Dedication

This book is dedicated to William D. (Don) Horton who served as a radio operator/gunner and also a bombardier in TBD-1 Devastators with VT-6 aboard USS ENTERPRISE, CV-6. During the pre-war years, Don usually flew as the bombardier or the radio operator/gunner in 6-T-2, and considered it "his" plane. At the Battle of Midway, he flew as the gunner in 6-T-5. After surviving the Battle of Midway, Don became a turret gunner in TBF Avengers, and he flew with the reformed VT-8 from USS HORNET, CV-8, at the Battle of the Santa Cruz Islands. He later served as a chief mechanic aboard USS SANGAMON, CVE-26. After the war, Don became a civilian representative with the U. S. Army's Missile Command (MICOM). In this capacity, he worked for author, Bert Kinzey, while both were assigned to the 3rd Battalion, 68th Air Defense Artillery (Hawk) at Homestead AFB, Florida. During the two years Don was assigned to this position, he spent many hours sharing his stories with the author and provided much technical information about the TBD-1 Devastator and TBF and TBM Avengers. Some of Don's comments appear in this book, and three aircraft in which he flew are illustrated in photographs and artwork.

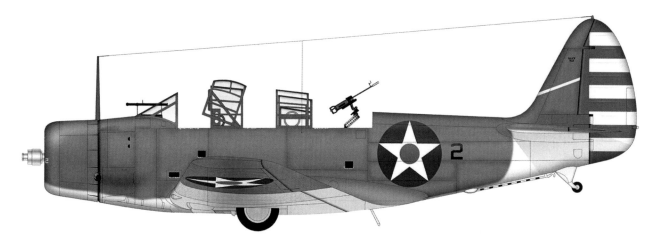

During the first half of 1942, TBD-1, BuNo. 1512, served as aircraft number 2 with VT-6. On February 1, it participated in the bombing attack at Wotje with Ensign T. A. Aspell as pilot, AOM2c R. L. Leonard as bombardier in the middle cockpit, and ARM2c W. D. Horton, to whom this book is dedicated, as gunner in the rear cockpit. A little over three weeks later, the same crew flew the Devastator during the bombing attack on Wake Island on February 24, however ARM2c Horton flew as the bombardier for that mission with AOM2c Leonard serving as the gunner. This TBD-1 would be lost during the Battle of Midway while being flown by Lt(jg) S. L. Rombach, with ARM3c W. F. Glenn as his gunner. Both were killed in the action. The profile above depicts how this aircraft looked during the bombing raids on Wotje and Wake Island in February 1942. At this time, U. S. Navy aircraft markings had evolved in an effort to make aircraft more readily identifiable by increasing the size of the national insignia to as large as practical and locating it in six positions rather than four. The red and white striped rudder was also added, and in the case of most VT-6 Devastators, only eleven stripes were used, rather than thirteen as often seen on other aircraft. However, these markings were relatively short lived, because the use of red caused confusion in combat with the markings on Japanese aircraft. (Artwork by Rock Roszak)

INTRODUCTION

An F4F-4 Wildcat displays the paint scheme and standard markings used by the U. S. Navy and Marine Corps in early 1942. Large national insignias are in all four wing positions and on both sides of the fuselage. Thirteen red and white stripes are on the rudder. This color photograph accurately depicts the colors in the Non-specular Blue-Gray over Light Gray paint scheme in new condition. In operational service, particularly on carriers, these colors weathered and faded considerably. (Grumman)

In 1922, the U. S. Navy converted the collier USS JUPITER to its first aircraft carrier and renamed the ship USS LANGLEY. Designated CV-1, LANGLEY became a test bed for the development of equipment, operating procedures, and aircraft that would be used on subsequent aircraft carriers. Landing an aircraft on a moving ship was no easy task to start with, but once it touched down on the flight deck, the best way to bring it to a safe stop was even more difficult to determine. Not only did the Navy have to develop arresting gear, catapults, and aircraft elevators, among many other details and concepts, it had to decide what types of aircraft would be assigned to its air groups. At that time, the Navy believed that the aircraft would be used as scouts to search for threats beyond the visual range of the fleet. If a threat was located, it would certainly be in the form of enemy ships, so other aircraft had to be included in the carrier's air group to attack those ships. Finally, assuming that other navies would develop aircraft carriers, the Navy realized that fighter aircraft would be needed to protect the fleet from both shipboard and land-based aircraft.

By 1927, the Navy's first two real aircraft carriers became operational when the converted battlecruisers, LEXINGTON, CV-2, and SARATOGA, CV-3, joined the fleet. The development of tactics, strategies, equipment, and aircraft continued into the 1930s, and the lessons learned formed the basis for safer and more effective operations. In 1933, USS RANGER, CV-4, was launched as the Navy's first aircraft carrier built as such from the keel up. By the time the Japanese attacked Pearl Harbor, three ships of a new class, including YORKTOWN, CV-5, ENTERPRISE, CV-6, and HORNET, CV-8, had joined the fleet along with the smaller WASP, CV-7. With LANGLEY having been converted to a seaplane tender, this left the U. S. Navy with seven aircraft carriers at the start of the war, but many more fleet, light, and escort carriers were already being built or were planned.

During the development of carrier-based air power, the Navy determined that the air groups would consist of three types of aircraft assigned to four types of squadrons. The aerial eyes of the fleet would be the scouts. As development evolved, these observation scouts were replaced by dive bombers as the eyes of the fleet. When armed with small bombs, they could patrol the seas for hundreds of miles around the fleet. When the enemy was found, or his location was already known, these same aircraft could be armed with heavier bomb loads and used to attack the target as dive bombers. By the time the U. S. entered World War II, these scout bombers were assigned to one scouting (VS) and one bombing (VB) squadron in each carrier. Although these squadrons had different names, they flew the same type of aircraft, and both squadrons trained for and flew both scouting and bombing missions. The designation for these aircraft included the letters "SB" for scout bomber:

The Navy believed that the single best weapon that an aircraft could use to attack a large enemy ship was the torpedo, so each carrier had a torpedo squadron (VT) assigned to the air group. The smaller RANGER and WASP had a limited number of these aircraft compared to the other larger carriers. Torpedo bombers could also carry a load of conventional free-fall bombs and serve in the role of horizontal bombers when attacking land targets. However, this was considered a secondary role, so torpedo bombers had the letters "TB" in their designations to indicate their type.

Finally, the Navy included a squadron of fighters in each carrier air group. These aircraft would defend the fleet from enemy carrier and land-based aircraft, and they would also fly with the scout and torpedo bombers to their targets to provide protection from enemy fighters.

By the time America entered World War II, this air group, consisting of a scouting squadron, a bombing squadron, a torpedo squadron, and a fighter squadron, was standard for the U. S. Navy's fleet carriers, and although the number of aircraft assigned to the various squadrons would change, these types of aircraft would remain operational aboard U. S. fleet carriers throughout the war. The smaller light and escort carriers operated composite air groups with various types of aircraft, but by 1943, these usually included Wildcat or Hellcat fighters and Avenger torpedo bombers. The four SANGAMON class escort carriers were the only American CVEs to operate dive bombers for any extended period of time during World War II.

The aircraft carrier RANGER and the four SANGAMON class escort carriers took part in the invasion of North Africa known as Operation Torch. This began on November 8, 1942. American carriers also saw limited action in other operations in the Atlantic and Mediterranean Sea, but their primary use in the Atlantic Theater was escorting convoys across the North Atlantic. Escort carriers provided constant air cover over the convoys, and what had begun as a shooting gallery for German U-boats became a grave yard for German submarines in the later years of the war. The use of both American and British escort carriers and improved use of increasing numbers of destroyer escorts insured that the vital lifelines between America and her allies in Europe remained open, thus providing the final victory over the Germans and Italians.

It was in the Pacific where the aircraft carrier ushered in an entire new age of naval warfare. At the Battle of the Coral Sea in May 1942, naval forces of the United States and Japan engaged each other without the surface ships ever coming in visual range of each other. This was a first in naval warfare, but it would happen many times thereafter during the remainder of the war. At Coral Sea, carrier based-aircraft provided the offensive punch that left one aircraft carrier sunk and another extensively damaged on each side. Only once in the entire Pacific war did American and Japanese battleships exchange gunfire in a surface battle reminiscent of those fought prior to the emergence of the aircraft carrier as the primary capital ship in the world's largest navies. Although other ship-to-ship combat did take place during the war in the Pacific, the primary and decisive naval battles were fought through the use of carrier-based aircraft on both sides. Joining the American carriers in this effort were aircraft carriers of the Royal Navy.

This publication takes a look at the carrier-based aircraft used by the United States Navy during World War II. Many of these were also flown by the Marines. It was these aircraft that projected the primary striking power of the U. S. Navy's surface forces in the Pacific during World War II. But the scope of the book is not limited to those aircraft that saw action during the war. Instead, we have included any aircraft that was operational with the Navy or Marines at any time during the war, and also those that were developed during the war, even if their introduction into service was too late to actually see combat. Examples of the latter include Grumman's F7F Tigercat and F8F Bearcat, and Ryan's FR-1 Fireball. All three of these aircraft did see operational service in the years following the war.

Also included are any designs developed during the war that made it at least to the flying prototype stage, even if they never became operational with fleet squadrons. Among these aircraft are the Bell XFL-1 Airabonita, Grumman XF5F-1 Skyrocket, Curtiss XF2R-1 Dark Shark as well as several others. Although they never saw operational service, their development and design features were often very interesting, and they led to advancements that were used in subsequent designs.

Concluding the book are two appendices that provide additional information which is pertinent to these carrier-based aircraft. Appendix 1 provides a summary of the major actions in the Pacific in which the carrier forces engaged, and maps show the location of each American and Japanese aircraft carrier that was lost. This appendix is divided into two time frames, one showing the earlier actions between December 7, 1941, when the United States entered the war with the Japanese attack on Pearl Harbor, and extending through August 1942. The second section covers the time period from August 1942 until VJ Day. This appendix points out how complete the destruction of the Japanese Navy was by the "awakened giant" following the attack on Pearl Harbor. The U. S. Navy only lost four fleet carriers during World War II, all during the first eleven months after the attack on Pearl Harbor. After the loss of USS HORNET, CV-8, on October 26, 1942, the United States never lost another fleet carrier during the war. Only one light carrier, USS PRINCETON, CVL-23, and five escort carriers were lost in the Pacific throughout the remaining three years of the war, and only one escort carrier was lost in the Atlantic. By comparison, every Japanese aircraft carrier was sunk or rendered out of action by war's end. Likewise, Japan lost eleven battleships, while American did not lose any battleships after the loss of USS ARIZONA and USS OKLAHOMA at Pearl Harbor. The destruction of Japan's capital ships and many other surface combatants was due in a large part to these carrier-based aircraft.

The second appendix provides a look at the paint schemes and markings that were used on U. S. carrier-based aircraft from the colorful-prewar years through the end of the war. New artwork, created specifically for this publication, illustrate these paint schemes and markings in considerable detail, and this information will be valuable to historians and scale modelers alike. In the late 1930s, Navy aircraft were brilliantly marked with yellow wings and colorful tails. War clouds on the horizon brought on the advent of camouflage for naval aircraft, and a succession of schemes evolved from overall gray to overall dark blue, with phases of intermediate blue and tri-color paint schemes in between. Naval aviation has always used a sophisticated system for marking aircraft in ways to identify the aircraft carrier to which they were assigned, but that became more difficult to do as the number of carriers dramatically increased from the seven carriers the United States had at the beginning of the war to the nearly one hundred fleet, light, and escort carriers operational by mid-1945.

For a detailed look at the Japanese attack on Pearl Harbor, see **Attack on Pearl Harbor, Japan Awakens A Sleeping Giant**. To learn more about his detailed and profusely illustrated publication, go online to this address: http://detailandscale.com/attack_on_pearl_harbor.html.

TBD-1, BuNo. 0323, was coded 6-T-2 and assigned to VT-6 during the pre-war period. It is shown here flying over its carrier, USS ENTERPRISE, CV-6. In the pre-war years, Don Horton, to whom this book is dedicated, regularly flew as the radio operator/gunner in this aircraft. Full color artwork of this aircraft is included elsewhere in this publication. Note the plane guard destroyer positioned behind the carrier. (NNAM)

Chapter 1

FIGHTERS

When the United States entered World War II in December 1941, Brewster F2A Buffalos remained in front line service in several Navy and Marine fighter squadrons. This F2A-3 taxis at Ewa Marine Corps Air Station just southwest of Pearl Harbor in early 1942. It was part of the air defense forces for Oahu in the early months of the war. It carries the red and white stripes on the rudder that were part of standard U. S. markings in early 1942. The large national insignia still has the red disc at the center, but this would eventually be deleted so as not to be confused with the Japanese insignia. (NNAM)

This chapter presents a look at the fighter aircraft types designed for the U. S. Navy and Marines immediately before and during World War II. All aircraft designs that made it to the flying prototype stage of development are included if they were designed or first flew during the war. Emphasis is placed on the four types that saw operational service in combat, these being the Brewster F2A Buffalo, Grumman's F4F Wildcat and F6F Hellcat, and Vought's F4U Corsair. Other fighters, including the F8F Bearcat, F7F Tigercat, and Ryan's FR-1 Fireball, also made it into service during the war, but they were too late to see combat before hostilities ended. Each of these fighter types is also illustrated with photographs and artwork, and the developmental history of each is summarized in the text and captions.

Also included is a brief look at each of the designs that flew but were never put into production or operational service. Of these, the XF5U-1 Flying Pancake, the XF-14C, and the XF-15C-1 Stingaree were some of the most unusual and unorthodox designs ever to fly. Boeing's huge XF8B-1 was never destined to be a fighter, but it foreshadowed the coming attack aircraft that first took the form of the A-1 Skyraider several years later.

When the Japanese attack at Pearl Harbor on December 7, 1941, brought America into the war, the primary fighter in Navy and Marine squadrons was the F4F Wildcat. Several squadrons were still equipped with Brewster's F2A Buffalo which would prove woefully inadequate against the Japanese at Midway in June 1942. For the next several months the Wildcat continued on as the only

The primary fighter in Navy and Marine squadrons when America entered World War II was Grumman's F4F-3 Wildcat. Subsequent versions of the Wildcat would remain in frontline service throughout World War II, serving in both the Atlantic and Pacific theaters. These F4F-3s were assigned to VF-5 aboard USS YORKTOWN, CV-5. They were painted in the overall Light Gray scheme which replaced the previous colorful markings in early 1941. The first number in the white fuselage code indicated that the aircraft were assigned to Fighter Squadron Five. The F stood for Fighter, and the last of the three characters was the aircraft's number within the squadron. (NNAM)

Grumman's F6F Hellcat was the most numerous of all U. S. Navy fighters in World War II. This large powerful aircraft could also carry a respectable bomb load, and later versions could also be armed with rockets. This meant that fighters could be a larger part of a carrier's air wing without reducing the ship's striking power. At the start of World War II, approximately twenty-five percent of the aircraft in each carrier's air wing were fighters, but at the end of the war, more than half of all aircraft aboard fleet and light carriers were the more capable heavy fighters, including the Hellcat and the Corsair. (NNAM)

fighter flown in combat by the Navy and Marine Corps. While it was not a match for Japanese fighters when it came to maneuverability, the Wildcat was rugged, dependable, and when flown using tactics designed to maximize its capabilities, it proved a worthy opponent for enemy fighters. Aces like Jimmy Thatch, Butch O'Hare, Joe Foss, and others ran up their scores against the more nimble Japanese aircraft and helped begin to turn the tide of battle by mid-1942.

In 1943, larger, heavier, and more powerful fighters entered the Navy and Marine inventories in the form of Grumman's F6F Hellcat and Vought's F4U Corsair. The Hellcat quickly replaced Wildcats in the squadrons aboard fleet and light carriers, but upgraded variants of the Wildcat continued to serve on escort carriers in both the Atlantic and Pacific theater for the entire war. Hell-

cats rapidly became the most numerous Navy fighter in the war, but Corsairs initially proved unsatisfactory for carrier operation. Early versions of the Corsair operated from island bases where they ran up impressive kill ratios over their Japanese opponents. Eventually, the problems relating to the Corsair's carrier suitability were solved, and more and more Corsairs were added to carrier air wings during the final year of the war.

The Hellcat and Corsair were much larger than the Wildcat, and they could be armed with bombs and rockets to attack ground targets. This meant that the percentage of fighters within carrier air wings was increased with each passing month of the war. By war's end, more than half of the aircraft assigned to fleet and light carriers were fighters. They not only flew the typical fighter missions of combat air patrols (CAP) to defend the fleet, and fighter

Vought's F4U Corsair was a superior fighter aircraft, being fast, well armed, and rugged. But early versions of the Corsair proved difficult to operate from carriers, so they were flown from island bases by Navy and Marine squadrons. This F4U-1 was assigned to the famous "Black Sheep" of VMF-214, a Marine squadron commanded by Major Gregory "Pappy" Boyington. It was photographed at the fighter strip on Esprito Santo on September 11, 1943. After changes were made, later versions of the Corsair operated effectively from aircraft carriers in the Pacific during the later stages of the war. (NNAM)

The F8F Bearcat was an effort to mate a powerful engine to the smallest possible airframe. This design was intended to create a fighter with a very high rate of climb that could be used to quickly intercept Japanese Kamikaze aircraft before they could attack U. S. ships. Several Navy squadrons transitioned to the Bearcat in 1945, but none made it to the combat zone before the war ended. This F8F is shown in the post-war years at NAS Oakland, California. (Munkasy collection)

escort to defend dive and torpedo bombers, they also played an important role in destroying land targets and attacking Japanese shipping at sea.

In the closing months of the war, new fighters were entering service with the Navy and Marines. These included the twin-engine F7F Tigercat, which like the Corsair, was not considered suitable for carrier operations. Tigercats were assigned to Marine squadrons, and a few of these reached Okinawa just as the war came to an end.

Another fighter to reach operational squadrons before the Japanese surrendered, but too late to see combat, was the F8F Bearcat. This small fighter was powered by the large Pratt & Whitney R-2800 radial also used in the much larger and heavier Hellcat and Corsair, thus giving it the best rate of climb of any propeller-driven fighter to enter service during the war. The Bearcat was designed specifically to be a fleet defense interceptor that could take off from a carrier and climb quickly to engage Kamikaze aircraft which were attacking the fleet. Bearcats continued in service after the war, but they were soon replaced by even faster jet fighters.

During World War II, a composite fighter, with both a radial engine and a small jet powerplant, was developed and became operational with the U. S. Navy. In March 1945, VF-66 flew carrier qualifications with the Ryan FR-1 Fireball. As with the Tigercat and Bearcat, Fireballs were too late to see combat, and they, along with the FR-2 Dark Shark and the Curtiss XF15C-1 Stingaree, both of which were also composite fighter designs, remain simply as an historic transitional step from propellers to turbojet engines as the means of propulsion for Navy and Marine Fighters.

A little known fact about Navy fighters of World War II is that an aircraft that was powered in part by a turbojet engine became operational and flew qualifications with a squadron aboard an aircraft carrier during the war. In March 1945, VF-66, took their Ryan FR-1 Fireball fighters to sea aboard USS RANGER, CV-4, for evaluations. The Fireball was one of three composite fighters developed for the Navy during the war, and it was powered by a radial piston engine and a small turbojet powerplant in the aft fuselage. The war ended before any Fireballs could be sent to the combat areas. (NNAM)

BREWSTER F2A BUFFALO

F2A-1, BuNo 1393, assigned to VF-3, noses up on the flight deck after a bad landing aboard USS SARATOGA, CV-3. The accident took place on March 11, 1940, and the aircraft was piloted by Jimmy Thach, who would become an innovative tactician and leader during World War II. The colorful pre-war markings on the Buffalo included silver paint applied to the fuselage and lower wing surfaces. The uppersurfaces of the wings were painted Chrome Yellow with diagonal stripes in the section color to which the aircraft was assigned, and these were usually outlined in black. The vertical and horizontal tail sections were painted a specific color depending on the aircraft carrier to which the plane was assigned. Different segments of the cowling were painted in various colors to denote the aircraft's position within the squadron. The national insignia was painted in all four wing positions, but it was not applied to the fuselage. See Appendix 2 for complete information on the paint schemes and markings used by Navy carrier-based aircraft during the war. (NNAM)

On June 22, 1936, the U. S. Navy placed an order with the Brewster Aeronautical Corporation for the prototype of a single-engine fighter that was to become the first shipboard monoplane fighter to enter service with Navy squadrons. Some references state that it was the first monoplane aircraft to enter service with the Navy, but that distinction goes to the Douglas TBD-1 Devastator torpedo bomber. Designated XF2A-1, the aircraft looked much like Brewster's XSBA-1 scout bomber that had been in development for almost two years. The new fighter was powered by a 950-horsepower Wright XR-1820-22 engine.

The sole XF2A-1, BuNo. 0451, made its first flight in December 1937, and then it was turned over to the U. S. Navy for testing. While evaluation of the new design continued, an order was placed for fifty-four F2A-1s, and deliveries began in June 1939. These first production aircraft were powered by a 940-horsepower R-1820-34 engine, and the vertical tail was enlarged. The canopy and windscreen were redesigned to provide better visibility, and the window in the bottom of the fuselage was also modified. Other

changes included moving the forward antenna mast from the left side of the fuselage to the right, and the landing light was repositioned from the left side of the forward fuselage to the underside of the left wing. A telescopic gun sight was added through the front glass plate of the windscreen. Armament consisted of one .50-caliber and one .30-caliber machine gun in the cowling. Provisions were made for two additional .50-caliber machine guns in the wings.

By the end of 1939, F2A-1s were being delivered to VF-3 aboard USS SARATOGA, CV-3, and by June 1940, the squadron was operating ten F2A-1s from the carrier. But only eleven F2A-1s were delivered to the Navy with the remainder of the contract for fifty-four aircraft being provided to Finland. These were called Model 239s, simply using the Brewster model number for the designation.

The XF2A-1 was again used as a prototype after being converted to the XF2A-2. An R-1820-40 engine with a new high-altitude carburetor increased output to 1,200 horsepower. The pro-

A right side view of F2A-1, BuNo. 1388, illustrates additional details of the pre-war markings used by VF-3 on their Buffalos. The fuselage is painted silver, and the top of the squadron's famous Felix the Cat marking is just visible on the fuselage above the wing. The fuselage code, 3-F-18, and a smaller U. S. NAVY are painted on the aft fuselage in black. The vertical and horizontal tail surfaces are painted white, indicating that the aircraft was assigned to USS SARATOGA, CV-3. The aircraft type and Bureau number are lettered on the rudder and vertical tail respectively in small black letters. The bottom half of the cowling is painted Lemon Yellow, indicating the third aircraft in Section 6 of the squadron. A thin black line separates the yellow lower part of the cowling from the upper silver section. (NNAM)

In December 1940, a directive was issued that officially replaced the colorful pre-war paint schemes with the low-visibility overall Light Gray scheme. This change began to take effect by February 1941. But prior to this change, the Navy experimented with a number of unusual camouflage designs. In September 1940, this F2A-1 was one of several Buffalos assigned to VF-3 that was painted in what was known as the McClelland Barclay camouflage designs. These did not prove to be very effective, so the overall Light Gray scheme was adopted for carrier-based aircraft instead. (USN)

peller was changed from a hydraulic to an electric system for pitch control, and a much larger spinner was placed over the hub. The R-1820-40 engine was bigger and 350 pounds heavier than the previous R-1820-34, so to maintain the correct center of balance, the forward fuselage was shortened by five inches. The cowling was redesigned, and the front opening was enlarged to increase the amount of cooling air flowing past the cylinders.

Once again, the Navy had to wait for its Buffalos, because the Roosevelt Administration ordered that forty Brewster Model 339Bs, the ground-based equivalent of the F2A-2, be delivered to Belgium first. After a six-month delay, the delivery of the forty-three production F2A-2s began to reach the fleet in September 1940. Eight of

the F2A-1s were also brought up to F2A-2 standards, giving the Navy a total of fifty-one Buffalos of this new variant. SARATOGA's VF-3 and LEXINGTON's VF-2 became operational in F2A-2s by the end of 1940.

F2A-2s were armed with four .50-caliber machine guns and two 100-pound bombs could be carried under the wings. Shortly after they entered service, the Navy ordered that the colorful pre-war markings be replaced with an overall Light Gray paint scheme. During operational service, pilots in VF-2 did not like the vibrations caused by the tall antenna mast on the forward fuselage, so they moved the forward mount for the antenna wire to a location on top of the left wing.

Colorful pre-war markings were applied to this F2A-2 from VF-2. This aircraft was assigned to USS LEXINGTON, CV-2, and had Lemon Yellow vertical and horizontal tail surfaces. (Artwork by Rock Roszak)

This F2A-2 is painted in the overall Light Gray scheme that was directed in December 1940, and which first appeared in February 1941. The F2A-2 could be distinguished from the F2A-1 by its larger spinner and because the openings in the cowling for the machine guns did not have fairings. The exhaust ports were also higher on the fuselage, and additional gas vents were added to each side of the forward fuselage. The F2A-2 had a more powerful Wright R-1820-40 engine which produced 1,200 horsepower, compared to only 950 horsepower with the R-1820-34 used in the F2A-1. This F2A-2 was assigned to the Carrier Transition Training Squadron at Oakland, California, in 1941. (NNAM)

As VF-2 and VF-3 gained experience with the Navy's first monoplane fighter, two problems developed. The R-1820-34 experienced bearing failures, so the engines needed constant attention. But more prevalent was the problem with the Buffalo's weak landing gear. It was not strong enough to withstand hard landings, and the main gear often failed, particularly when operating aboard aircraft carriers. Although Brewster modified the main gear to make it stronger, failures continued to plague the Buffalo throughout its service life.

In January 1941, the Navy placed an order for 108 F2A-3s. This final production version of the Buffalo featured a longer forward fuselage which was extended ten inches in front of the leading edge of the wing. Armor protection was provided for the pilot, the fuel capacity was increased, and more ammunition could be carried for the four .50-caliber machine guns. This increased the weight of the F2A-3 considerably over that of the F2A-2, and performance suffered accordingly. The F2A-3 could easily be identi-

fied from the two earlier Buffalo variants, because no spinner was mounted on the propeller hub.

Even by the time the F2A-3 was ordered, the Navy had decided that Grumman's new F4F-3 was clearly a superior fighter, and F2As only equipped VF-2, VF-3, and VS-201, the latter operating aboard the Navy's first escort carrier, USS LONG ISLAND. Other Buffalos were assigned to training squadrons, while some F2A-2s and F2A-3s were turned over to Marine squadrons.

By the time the Japanese attacked Pearl Harbor, VF-2 was the only Navy fighter squadron (VF) still flying Buffalos, and these were replaced by F4F-3s by the end of January 1942. VS-201 was the last operational Navy squadron to fly the Buffalo, but by April 1942, all of its F2A-3s had been transferred to training units or to the Marines.

Marine fighter squadron VMF-221 was based on Midway Island, and it was the only U. S. squadron to see any real combat with the Buffalo. Four if its F2A-3s intercepted a Japanese "Emily"

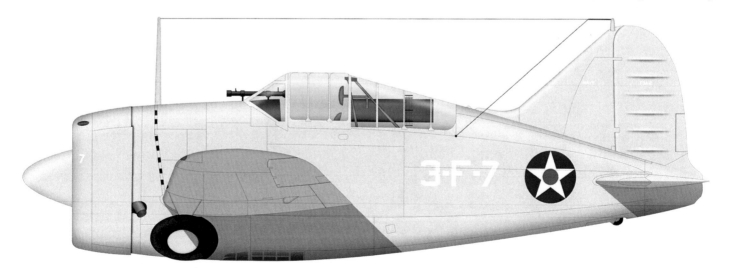

This F2A-2 was assigned to VF-3 aboard USS SARATOGA, CV-3, in 1941, and is painted in the overall Light Gray scheme. The smaller national insignia is evident and was only located in four positions. The code 3-F-7 indicates it was aircraft number seven in Fighting THREE. (Artwork by Rock Roszak)

In May 1942, F2A-3s were still serving in front line squadrons with the Marine Corps. Some were part of the defenses of the military facilities on Oahu, including Pearl Harbor. Here an F2A-3 of VMF-221 is serviced under the trees at Ewa MCAS, located just to the southwest of Pearl Harbor. The Buffalo is painted in the Blue-Gray over Light Gray scheme, and note that the red disc at the center of the national insignia and the red and white stripes on the rudder were still in use at this time. The Marine air station had been attacked by the Japanese on December 7, 1941, and almost all of the aircraft based there at that time were either destroyed or severely damaged. (NNAM)

flying boat on March 10,1942, and they shot the four-engine patrol plane down as it flew a reconnaissance mission near Midway. This was the first American aerial victory scored in a Buffalo.

At the decisive Battle of Midway, VMF-221 did not fare as well. On June 4, 1942, the squadron's strength report included seven F4F Wildcats and twenty-one F2A-3s. As the Japanese aircraft attacked, twenty F2A-3s and five F4Fs, under the command of Major Floyd B. "Red" Parks, rose to meet the enemy. Thirteen of the Buffalos and two Wildcats were shot down. Japanese losses were two A6M2 Zero fighters and seven B5N2 Kate attack bombers.

This was the Buffalo's only significant combat in the hands of American pilots. The aircraft itself has received much of the blame for its poor showing, but it must also be understood that a third of VMF-221's pilots were right out of flight school, and they were flying against the best pilots in the Imperial Japanese Navy. Further, they were severely outnumbered, so everything was against the American defenders as soon as they took off to meet the Japanese carrier strike force.

The last operational American squadron to fly the Buffalo was VMF-211 which was based on Palmayra Island. This unit also flew from the escort carrier USS LONG ISLAND, AVG-1. The designation for the ship was later changed to CVE-1. In late summer 1942, VMF-211 finally sent its Buffalos back to the mainland where they were used in training units throughout the rest of the war.

Brewster Model 239s and 339s, as they were called in foreign service, fared somewhat better in combat for other nations. As stated previously, Finland received forty-three F2A-1s originally slated for service with the U. S. Navy. These were designated Model 239s, and they performed well against Soviet aircraft, shooting down 496 enemy aircraft while losing only nineteen Model 239s.

Forty Model 339Bs, land-based counterparts of the F2A-2, were supplied to Belgium, and of these, thirty-three were subsequently sent to England. Great Britain also received 170 Model 339Es which they designated Buffalo Mk 1s. Twenty-four Model 339Cs and forty-eight Model 339Ds were provided to the Dutch East Indies. Seventeen Buffalos, designated Model 339-23, also served without seeing combat with the Royal Australian Air Force.

This F2A-3 is shown in the markings believed to have been used by Major "Red" Parks while the commander of VMF-221. Parks went missing in action in the defense of Midway Island on the morning June 4th, 1942. (Artwork by Rock Roszak)

Right: This photo shows the crash of an F2A-3 assigned to VMF-211 aboard USS LONG ISLAND, AVG-1 (later redesignated CVE-1), off Palmayra Island on July 25, 1942. VMF-211 was the last front line Marine fighter squadron to operate the Buffalo. (NNAM)

Below: By the second half of 1942, all Buffalos had been replaced in front line squadrons, but some remained in service as trainers. This F2A-3 was assigned to the training unit at Miami, Florida, and when this photo was taken, it was being flown by Lt Cdr. J. C. "Jumpin' Joe" Clifton. Clifton would go on to be an outstanding leader during World War II, commanding VF-12, Air Group 12, and later USS WASP, CV-18. Following the war, he rose to the rank of rear admiral, and today the Joseph C. Clifton award for meritorious service by a fighter squadron while deployed aboard a carrier is named in his honor. (NNAM)

GRUMMAN F4F & GENERAL MOTORS FM WILDCAT

The XF4F-2 was the first prototype of the Wildcat series. Note the machine gun barrel protruding from the cowling and the dual windows under the wing. Although the basic design of the Wildcat was established with this aircraft, it differed considerably from production aircraft in that it had rounded tips on the wings and all tail surfaces. (Grumman)

What was to become one of the most important fighter aircraft of World War II actually began as a biplane design. Designated the XF4F-1 and ordered on March 2, 1936, it was intended to be a back-up in the event its monoplane competitor, the Brewster XF2A-1, failed to meet expectations. Even before either aircraft was built, analysis of the two designs showed conclusively that the XF2A-1 would offer much better performance than the biplane. Further, the XF4F-1 promised little increase in performance over the existing Grumman F3F-3 biplane fighter then in service.

To better compete with the Brewster XF2A-1, Grumman went back to the drawing board and came up with a reworked monoplane design which was ordered by the Navy on July 28, 1936, as the XF4F-2. The mid-wing monoplane was powered by a 1,050-horsepower Pratt & Whitney R-1830-66 Twin Wasp engine that promised a top speed of almost three hundred miles-per-hour. Internal armament consisted of two .50-caliber machine guns in the cowling and two more in the wings. Provisions were made to carry two 100-pound bombs under the wings, however, the wings were not designed to fold to save space on aircraft carriers. The retractable main gear was a holdover from previous Grumman designs. It was manually cranked up and down by the pilot using a handle that turned a series of gears and chains similar to that found on a bicycle. Once retracted, the main gear wheels fit nearly flush with the sides of the forward fuselage.

The XF4F-2 made its first flight on September 2, 1937, but all was not well with the design. In a competition with the Brewster XF2A-1, the XF4F-2 lost out, and Grumman engineers went back to work once again to improve the aircraft.

In October 1938, the Navy contracted for a reworked prototype designated the XF4F-3. This was powered by an XR-1830-76 engine with a two-stage, two-speed supercharger. The rounded tips of the wings and tail surfaces were replaced with blunt tips, and the fuselage was also redesigned. Armament was two .30-caliber machine guns in the cowling and two .50-caliber weapons in the wings. The first flight of the XF4F-3 was made on February

12, 1939, and top speed was recorded as 333 miles-per-hour, a substantial increase over the 290 mph achieved by the XF4F-2. Although several problems remained to be solved, particularly that of engine cooling, the Navy placed an order for fifty-four production F4F-3s in August 1939. Delivery of these began reaching the Navy in February 1940.

The first two F4F-3s retained the same mixed-caliber machine gun armament in the cowling and wings as the XF4F-3, but all subsequent F4F-3s had four .50-caliber machine guns in the wings. The first of these two F4F-3s was sent to NACA's Langley facility in Virginia to study ways to improve engine cooling. The second was retained by Grumman as a test aircraft. The third and fourth F4F-3s had Wright R-1820-40 engines installed and were redesignated XF4F-5 and XF4F-6 respectively. Deliveries of Wildcats to U. S. Navy squadrons began with the fifth production F4F-3.

Production F4F-3s also had a redesigned tail section with a curved fillet blending the leading edge of the vertical tail with the

The XF4F-3 was more like the production aircraft that followed. It had blunt tips on the wings and tail surfaces, and the canopy was redesigned to what would become production standards. The horizontal tail remained mounted on the fuselage. This aircraft was later modified to early production standards. (Grumman)

The second production F3F-3 still has the machine guns mounted in the cowling, but the tail is now what would become standard on production aircraft. The horizontal stabilizer and elevators have been moved to a low position on the vertical tail, and the vertical stabilizer and rudder have been redesigned. (Grumman)

The Navy experimented with fitting floats to several different types of aircraft just prior to America's entry into World War II. These included this F4F-3 Wildcat, which was designated the F4F-3S and called the Wildcatfish. The other aircraft that were tested with floats included an SB2U-1 Vindicator, a TBD-1 Devastator, and later an SB2C-1 Helldiver. Note how the main landing gear wells on the F4F-3S were covered over. Small fins were added to the horizontal stabilizers to provide increased directional stability necessitated by the addition of the floats. (NNAM)

spine of the fuselage. The horizontal tail was moved from a position on the fuselage to a low-mounted position on the vertical tail. Early F4F-3s were powered by a Pratt & Whitney R-1830-76 engine, but this was later changed to the R-1830-86. Some Wildcats were delivered with R-1830-90 engines, and these were designated F4F-3As.

As war clouds grew on the horizon, the Navy was concerned that it might not have enough aircraft carriers once hostilities began with Japan. The potential loss of carriers in combat could compound this problem. As a possible solution, the Navy experimented with fitting floats to several different types of carrier-based aircraft, so that they could be operated from remote areas where there were no landing fields. Experiments were conducted with two SB2U Vindicators, a TBD-1 Devastator, and later an SB2C-1 Helldiver, all of which were fitted with floats. One F4F-3, BuNo. 4038, was also fitted with floats and called the F4F-3S Wildcatfish. But after the Battle of Midway, and with the Navy's construction battalions (CBs) proving they could turn jungles into airfields quickly anywhere in the Pacific, the floatplane experiments ended without any production examples being ordered. The Japanese did develop and use floatplane fighters during the war.

A second production order for F4F-3s was placed, and during 1940 and 1941, Wildcats began to replace older types in both Navy and Marine squadrons. By December 1941, when the Japanese

The era of colorful pre-war paint schemes and markings was coming to an end as the F4F-3 was entering service, and only a very few were painted in the bright colors. One of the few remaining F4F-3s is now on display at the National Naval Aviation Museum aboard NAS Pensacola, Florida. It is accurately marked as a Wildcat assigned to VF-72 aboard USS WASP, CV-7, as indicated by the black tail. (Kinzey)

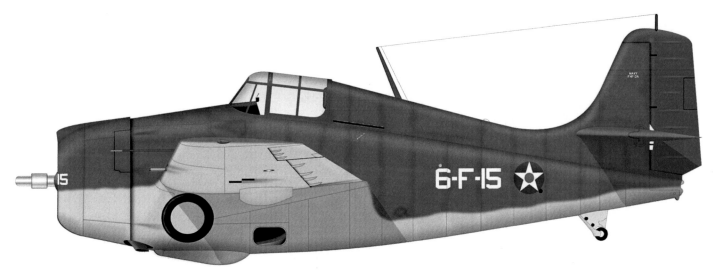

F4F-3 Wildcat, 6-F-15, flown by Ensign Herbert H. Menges of Fighting Squadron SIX (VF-6) aboard USS ENTERPRISE after the Japanese attack on Pearl Harbor. Ensign Menges was one of six Wildcat pilots who escorted the eighteen TBD-1 Devastators and six SBD-2 Dauntlesses on the mission to attack the two Japanese aircraft carriers reported south of Oahu. After finding nothing, the Devastators and Dauntlesses returned to ENTERPRISE, but the six fighters flew in to land at Ford Island. As they approached, Ensign Menges was immediately shot down by friendly anti-aircraft guns, becoming the first Navy fighter pilot to die in the Pacific War. Four of the six Wildcats were shot down by U. S. forces that night, and three of the pilots were killed. Fighting SIX still had white fuselage codes on its Wildcats on December 7, 1941, while the other squadrons in the ENTER-PRISE air group had changed to black fuselage codes. (Artwork by Rock Roszak)

attacked Pearl Harbor, Wildcats were the most numerous fighter in service with the Navy and Marines. They were quickly pressed into action against the more maneuverable Japanese fighters, and American pilots went through a quick learning process. Although unable to outmaneuver the lighter Japanese fighters, pilots like Jimmy Thatch, Butch O'Hare, Joe Foss, and others designed tactics to optimize the Wildcats strong points while putting the Japanese at a disadvantage. The success of their efforts was born out in the skies over the Pacific throughout 1942 and much of 1943 when the Wildcat remained the best fighter available to the Navy and Marines.

Interviews with Wildcat pilots revealed that none of them wanted to trade their sturdy Grumman aircraft for the more nimble Japanese fighters. Although they were more maneuverable, the Japanese fighters had little in the way of armor protection, and once hit,

they could withstand little damage. They often burst into flames and fell out of the sky after receiving a relatively small burst of fire from American fighters. But the Wildcat was rugged, and it seldom caught fire when hit. It often brought its pilot safely back home with considerable damage, and this was a feature the pilots loved.

Wildcats operated from both carriers and land bases during the first two years of the war, and they played key roles in the battles at Coral Sea, Midway, and Guadalcanal. Several pilots began to run up their scores against the Japanese, and the first Navy and Marine aces emerged.

In the spring of 1942, even before the Battle of Midway took place, the F4F-4 had begun to replace the F4F-3, and by summer, most front line Navy and Marine squadrons were equipped with the new variant. An important feature that appeared with the F4F-4 was that the wings could be folded back along the fuselage so

The F4F-4 was the first version of the Wildcat to feature folding wings which made it more suitable for carrier operations. The wings folded to little more than the span of the horizontal tail. Wildcats easily operated from even the smallest escort carriers. (NNAM)

15

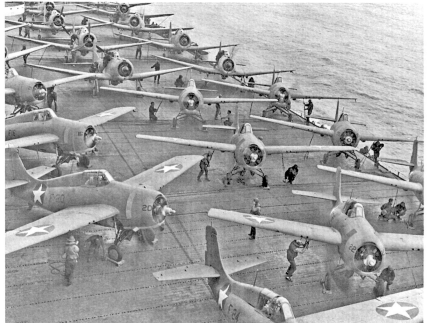

When the Battle of Midway took place in June 1942, the red and white stripes had been removed from the rudder, and the red disc at the center of the national insignia had also been deleted, thus leaving no red at all in the U. S. markings to be confused with the Japanese insignia. F4F-4s assigned to VF-8 aboard USS HORNET, CV-8, warm up their engines prior to launching on a strike against the Japanese carrier force on the morning of June 4. (NNAM)

U. S. Marine Corps F4F-4s from VMF-121 are ready to launch from one of the fighter strips on Guadalcanal in late 1942. The Wildcat in the foreground carries an external fuel tank under the fuselage, while the one in the background has a single tank under the right wing. U. S. Army P-38 Lightnings are sharing the strip with the Wildcats. (U. S. Navy)

that more aircraft could be stored aboard an aircraft carrier. The long pitot probe on the leading edge of the left wing had to be changed to a much shorter cranked probe under the wing tip to keep it from hitting the ground or carrier deck when folded.

Another noteworthy change on the F4F-4 was that the internal armament was increased from four to six .50-caliber machine guns, but this was not popular with many pilots. They preferred the four guns and more ammunition so they could fire for a longer time. In the F4F-4, the six guns had far less ammunition per gun, and although the firepower was increased, the firing duration was decreased.

The most unusual of the Wildcat variants to reach production status was the F4F-7. Twenty-one were built as long-range pho-

Below: U. S. Navy Wildcats also operated from Guadalcanal. This F4F-4 was assigned to the "Sundowners" of VF-11 when the squadron was stationed on the island in June 1943. The aircraft is illustrated as it appeared on June 12th after Lt(jg) William Leonard shot down two Zeros on that date. (Artwork by Rock Roszak)

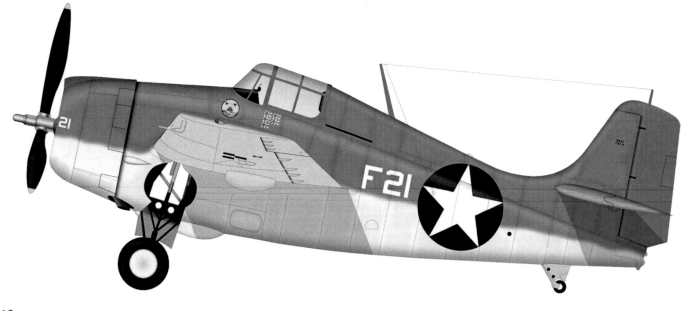

F4F-4 COCKPIT DETAILS

A reflector gunsight was used to aim the six .50-caliber machine guns of the F4F-4. It was mounted above the instrumental panel behind the forward bulletproof glass of the windscreen. (Kinzey)

The only surviving F4F-4 is on display at the Marine Corps Museum at Quantico, Virginia. The cockpit is beautifully restored, and only the turn-and-bank indicator is missing from the center of the main panel. The hole beneath the radio compass on the center pedestal was for cockpit ventilation. (Kinzey)

The cockpit was covered by a sliding canopy which remained unchanged on all Wildcat versions. A circular padded headrest was located above the seat. Armor plate protected the pilot from behind. The metal seats were often painted Interior Green, but it was not uncommon to find black seats in Wildcats. (Kinzey)

The engine and propeller controls were mounted on the black quadrant, while the bomb release handles were on the silver quadrant farther forward and lower on the left side of the cockpit. The silver lever with the red handle is the supercharger control, and the large white circular item is the landing gear warning horn. (Kinzey)

The electrical distribution panel was mounted high on the right side of the cockpit. The black hand crank, used to raise and lower the main landing gear, was just below it, and circuit breaker reset buttons were on the lower black panel. Radio controls were on the box aft of the electrical distribution panel. (Kinzey)

The F4F-7 was a long-range reconnaissance version of the Wildcat based on the F4F-3. It had the F4F-3's rigid wings, but no guns were installed. Instead, additional fuel tanks were added, bringing the total capacity up to 555 gallons. To dump fuel quickly, two fuel dump tubes were added just below the base of the rudder. The windscreen was also modified to a more rounded shape, and it was larger than those on F4F-3s. Twenty-one F4F-7s were built. (Grumman)

tographic reconnaissance aircraft, and they were based on the F4F-3's airframe. These Wildcats had the same rigid wing as the F4F-3, but no guns were installed. Instead, they were filled with fuel tanks. A total of 555 gallons of fuel could be carried internally allowing the F4F-7 to fly for up to twenty-five hours while covering more than 4,500 miles. To reduce pilot fatigue on these long flights, an autopilot was installed. The windscreen was more rounded and was larger than the one found on other Wildcat variants, and no armor protection was installed. Cameras were fitted in the rear fuselage. At least two of these reconnaissance Wildcats saw service during the fighting at Guadalcanal. An additional 100 F4F-7s were ordered, but the contract was changed before production began, and these aircraft were delivered as standard F4F-3s instead.

As the war continued, Grumman's attention was occupied with the development and production of the F6F Hellcat and later the F7F Tigercat and F8F Bearcat. It was decided that production of

the F4F Wildcat and TBF Avenger should be moved to General Motor's Eastern Aircraft Division. Wildcats produced by Eastern became known as FM-1s and FM-2s, while Avengers were designated TBMs.

Although it was being replaced by the F6F Hellcat and F4U Corsair in many squadrons, the Navy wanted to continue production of the Wildcat. Its small size and great handling capabilities made it an excellent fighter for the small escort carriers operating in both the Atlantic and Pacific. In the Atlantic, it teamed up with TBM Avengers aboard escort carriers to provide an air umbrella over convoys moving between the United States and Europe. In the Pacific, it provided air support to Army and Marine units on the ground as well as flying anti-submarine patrols near the fleet.

The FM-1 was essentially the same as the F4F-4, except that it was armed with only four machine guns instead of six. This pleased many pilots who had preferred the four-gun armament of the F4F-3 over the six-gun arrangement in the F4F-4. The four

An FM-1 assigned to VC-1 takes off from USS KASAAN BAY, CVE-69, on February 6, 1944. It is painted in the tri-color scheme. The FM-1 was essentially an F4F-4 built by the Eastern Aircraft Division of General Motors, with the exception that it was only armed with four .50-caliber machine guns instead of six. (U. S. Navy)

This FM-1 is being maneuvered on the flight deck of USS BLOCK ISLAND, CVE-21, after becoming entangled in the barriers. It is painted in the Dark Gull Gray over white paint scheme commonly used in the Atlantic. The national insignias have the red surround. (NNAM)

An FM-2 from VC-95 recovers aboard USS PETROF BAY, CVE-80, in 1945. Since this escort carrier operated in the Pacific, the Wildcat is painted in the overall Sea Blue scheme. Aircraft from this carrier had a white clover leaf painted on their vertical tails. Note the FM-2's taller vertical tail that was necessary to counter the torque of the more powerful Wright R-1820-56 engine. (NNAM)

guns were supplied with 1,720 rounds of ammunition which increased the firing duration considerably over the F4F-4. But only 839 FM-1s were delivered before production moved on to the more powerful FM-2. Many FM-1s served in the Atlantic on escort carriers, while others were assigned to training units.

The FM-2 was a much improved version of the Wildcat. It was powered by a Wright Cyclone R-1820-56 engine which produced 1,350 horsepower. To counter the torque of the more powerful engine, the vertical tail and rudder had to be increased in height. A total of 4,437 FM-2s were delivered, making it the most numerous Wildcat variant by far and exceeding the total number of all other Wildcat variants combined. As with the FM-1, armament remained four .50-caliber machine guns, but FM-2s were often

seen carrying rockets to attack surface ships, submarines, and land targets. Zero-length rocket launch stubs were added as a standard feature during FM-2 production. FM-2s operated aboard escort carriers until the end of the war, making the Wildcat one of the few American aircraft to serve in front line squadrons throughout the entire war.

It should be noted that the Wildcat was ordered by the French Navy in 1939 as the G-36A, but France surrendered to Germany before deliveries could be made. Almost 1,100 Wildcats in six different variants served with the Royal Navy during World War II. However, the aircraft was called the Martlet in RN service until January 1944, when the British decided to use the American name, Wildcat.

This FM-2 was assigned to VC-83 aboard the escort carrier USS SARGENT BAY, CVE-83, and the artwork illustrates the Wildcat as it appeared in May 1945. (Artwork by Rock Roszak)

FM-2 COCKPIT DETAILS

Although the instrument panel in the FM-2 was similar to that found in earlier Wildcat variants, there were some differences. A Mk VIII illuminated gunsight was installed above the instrument panel. The red handle to the right controlled the position of the cowl flaps. (Kinzey)

Details of the control column and center pedestal are shown here. A valve to control cockpit ventilation air was on the front of the pedestal. Wildcats did hot have floors in the cockpit. Instead, the pilot's feet were positioned on troughs below the rudder pedals. (Kinzey)

For the most part, the items on the left console remained the same as they had been on previous Wildcat variants. The red handle at the aft end of the console was the fuel selector valve, and the red lever forward of it was the flap control. Engine controls were on the throttle quadrant, and aft of it was the pitch trim control. (Kinzey)

The electrical distribution panel remained the primary feature on the right side of the cockpit, and below it was the circuit breaker panel. Controls for the radios were directly above it. Even on the FM-2, the landing gear was operated by a manual hand crank located below the aft end of the electrical distribution panel. (Kinzey)

XFL-1 AIRABONITA

Design similarities between the XFL-1 and the P-39 are readily apparent in this flying view of the Airabonita. The fuselage and tail surfaces were painted silver, as were the undersides of the wings. The upper surfaces of the wings were yellow, and the large national insignia was in all four wing positions. (NNAM)

On November 8, 1938, the Navy ordered a single XFL-1 prototype of a carrier fighter based on Bell's P-39 Airacobra. Although there were numerous design similarities between the P-39 and the XFL-1, the Airabonita, as it became known, was not simply a modified Airacobra. It had a wingspan that was a foot longer than the P-39, and wing area was increased by approximately nineteen square feet to improve slow speed handling. More noticeable was the fact that the XFL-1 featured a conventional landing gear rather than the tricycle layout used on all Airacobra variants.

The first flight of the XFL-1 took place on May 13, 1940, and the aircraft was powered by an Allison XV-1710-6 engine that produced 1,150 horsepower.

The Navy had some concerns about the Airabonita, and among these was that the engine was placed behind the cockpit.

A crash aboard a carrier could cause the engine to break loose from its mounts and be thrown forward inside the fuselage, thus crushing the pilot. Further, it was feared that the two automobile type doors would be difficult to open against water pressure if the aircraft ditched at sea.

Flight testing revealed longitudinal stability problems that had to be corrected by enlarging the vertical tail. Landing gear failures also plagued the test program, and the aircraft was deemed unsuitable for carrier operations.

With the development of Vought's large and powerful XF4U-1 already underway, the Navy did not see a need for the Airabonita, and the program was rather unceremoniously canceled without any orders being placed for production aircraft.

Unlike the P-39 Airacobra, the Airabonita had a conventional landing gear, because it was considered a better choice for carrier operations at that time. Note the very small scoop just aft of the canopy on the spine of the fuselage. The XFL-1 was the last Navy aircraft delivered with vertical red, white, and blue stripes on the rudder. These were subsequently removed. (NNAM)

This later photograph shows the XFL-1 with the rudder stripes removed. Also note that the air scoop directly aft of the canopy is larger in this photograph, and it looks more like the one that was standard on production Airacobras. (NNAM)

XF5F-1 SKYROCKET

The XF5F-1 Skyrocket flies in its original configuration. Note that the nose does not extend forward of the leading edge of the wing. The fuselage, engine nacelles, and underside of the wing were painted silver, while the top surface of the wing was painted yellow. (NNAM)

In the late 1930s, everyone in the U. S. armed forces knew war was coming. It was just a matter of time. Within tight budget constraints, every possible new weapon was studied, and developments in aviation were experiencing rapid advances as military aircraft moved from the biplane era to the age of the monoplane. Numerous new designs were studied, but none was more ambitious than Grumman's twin-engine fighter designated the XF5F-1 by the Navy. At a time when no monoplane had yet entered operational service, Grumman received a contract for one prototype for the twin-engine monoplane fighter on June 30, 1938.

The first flight of the Skyrocket, as it was dubbed by Grumman, was made on April 1, 1940, but several problems were noted during the flight testing. There was insufficient cooling for the two Wright XR-1820 engines, and the unusual design caused forward and downward visibility problems for the pilot. Poor stability was another concern.

In an attempt to correct the problems, Grumman made numerous changes to the XF5F-1. These included lowering the cockpit, extending the nose forward of the leading edge of the wing, redesigning the main landing gear doors, and extending the engine nacelles aft past the trailing edge of the wing. Spinners were also mounted to the propeller hubs.

Flight testing resumed in the summer of 1941, but problems remained, and the Navy did not place an order for production Skyrockets. Likewise, a variant for the U. S. Army, designated the XP-50, was tested, but the project was canceled. Nevertheless, the twin-engine design showed promise, and the XF5F-1 continued to fly as a test bed until December 1944. Lessons learned were applied to the development of the twin-engine F7F Tigercat which entered service just as the war was ending. The XF5F-1 Skyrocket remains the only monoplane fighter developed by Grumman that was not named for a member of the cat family.

The XF5F-1 was later modified with a longer nose and large spinners on the propeller hubs. Although it is difficult to see in this view, the cockpit was lowered on the redesigned XF5F-1. The engine nacelles were also lengthened so that they extended farther aft. (NNAM)

Grumman also produced a version of the Skyrocket with a longer nose and a tricycle landing gear. Designated the XP-50, this aircraft was intended for use by the Army Air Corps, but the project was abandoned after only twenty flying hours. (NNAM)

VOUGHT F4U, GOODYEAR FG, & BREWSTER F3A CORSAIR

Only one XF4U-1 prototype, BuNo. 1443, was built. It made its first flight on May 29, 1940, but it crash landed on a golf course on its fifth flight. It was rebuilt over a period of two months, and flight testing continued. On October 1, 1940, it made history when it became the first U. S. fighter to exceed 400 miles-per-hour in level flight. Note the original design of the canopy. (Vought)

On June 30, 1938, the same day that Grumman received the contract for the XF5F-1 Skyrocket, Vought Corporation was awarded a contract for a new single-engine carrier-based fighter. One prototype, designated the XF4U-1, was authorized, and a team of engineers lead by Rex B. Beisel created a design with some rather unusual characteristics. Most noteworthy was the inverted gull wing, a feature which would later earn the fighter one of its many nicknames; "bent wing bird." The inverted gull wing meant that the main landing gear struts could be kept strong and short while still providing plenty of clearance for the large propeller which had a diameter of more than thirteen feet. To turn this huge propeller, the supercharged Pratt & Whitney XR-2800-4 engine

The XF4U-1 is shown here as it appeared on April 19, 1941, after it was rebuilt following its crash. The prototype was armed with two .30-caliber machine guns in its cowling with 750 rounds of ammunition for each. Two .50-caliber machine guns were installed in the wings, and 300 rounds were provided for each of these guns. An unusual feature was that forty 5.2-pound, anti-aircraft, fragmentation bombs could be carried inside compartments in the wings. The idea was for the pilot to fly above an enemy bomber formation and drop these bombs into it. (Vought)

was selected. At 1,800 horsepower, it was the most powerful engine then available.

Another unusual feature of the prototype consisted of small compartments under the wings which were designed to hold forty small fragmentation bombs. These were to be dropped over bomber formations to explode among the enemy aircraft. This rather novel feature was not included on production Corsairs.

Most fighter designs of the late 1930s included machine guns in the cowling, and in this respect, the XF4U-1 was no different. It had two .30-caliber machine guns in the cowling with 750 rounds of ammunition per gun, and two .50-caliber weapons in the wings with 300 rounds of ammunition per gun. As was also the case with other fighters of this time period, the cowl guns would later be deleted and replaced with heavier wing armament on production aircraft.

On May 29, 1940, the XF4U-1 made its first flight from Vought's facility at Stratford, Connecticut. Shortly thereafter, on the aircraft's fifth flight, Boone T. Guyton found himself short of fuel and made an emergency landing on a golf course at Norwich. The aircraft flipped over on its back, tearing off the right wing and crushing the tail section in the process. This disaster could have ended the program that would produce one of the best and most versatile fighters of all time, but fortunately, Vought was able to salvage the XF4U-1 and repair it so that flight testing could be continued.

By October 1, 1940, the prototype was flying again, and it made aviation history by becoming the first U. S. fighter to exceed 400 miles-per-hour in level flight. This remarkable feat caught the eye of the Army Air Corps, and General "Hap" Arnold ordered the Army to take a look at the powerful new Pratt & Whitney engine. This would eventually lead to the development of the large rugged P-47 Thunderbolt which was also powered by the R-2800.

As Vought continued to work out some handling problems, and Pratt & Whitney tried to solve issues relating to engine cooling, the Navy ordered 584 production F4U-1s on June 30, 1941.

23

This photograph shows an F4U-1 from the "Jolly Rogers" of VF-17 landing aboard USS BUNKER HILL, CV-17, during qualifications in June and July 1943. The early problem with the Corsair dropping off onto its left wing when landing is readily apparent. The aft position of the cockpit made forward visibility over the long nose less than desirable for carrier operations. As a result, VF-17 and other Corsair squadrons were initially assigned to land bases. (U. S. Navy)

But another year passed before the first of these flew on June 25, 1942. By then the design had been modified to solve some of the problems. The cockpit had been moved aft thirty-two inches to make room for a 237-gallon fuel tank in the forward fuselage. Two tanks in the center wing section were deleted. The relocation of the cockpit would severely restrict forward visibility and lead in part to the F4U-1 being considered unsuitable for carrier operations. Other changes included the removal of the cowl guns, and six .50-caliber machine guns became the standard armament for the production aircraft. Likewise, the provisions for the small fragmentation bombs were eliminated. Instead, small racks to carry 100-pound bombs were added under the wings. Armor protection and self-sealing fuel tanks were added, the tail gear and arresting hook were redesigned, as was the canopy enclosure. The span of the ailerons was increased, and the deflector plate flaps were changed to a slotted design. Finally, the R-2800-4 engine was replaced with a R-2900-8 which developed 2,000 horsepower.

Carrier trials were flown in September 1942 aboard the escort carrier USS SANGAMON, CVE-26, but several problems were noted. Visibility was not good, and the left wing tended to stall before the right wing, causing the aircraft to slam down on the flight deck when landing. These problems were again noted when VF-17 flew carrier qualifications aboard USS BUNKER HILL, CV-17, in June and July of 1943. As a result, F4U-1s were assigned to land-based Marine and Navy squadrons.

Except for its difficulties operating from carriers, the Corsair proved to be an outstanding fighter. To increase deliveries, the Navy ordered Goodyear to open a production line building identical aircraft designated FG-1s. Brewster also began building a version without folding wings designated the F3A-1. However, the Brewster Corsairs proved to be less than satisfactory, and they were used only in training squadrons within the United States.

To improve visibility, two changes were introduced on the F4U-1A. These included a new semi-bubble canopy and a tail gear strut that was lengthened 6.48 inches. While the canopy change was made from the start of F4U-1A production, the tail strut change was not made until BuNo. 50080. This raised the tail, and therefore lowered the nose, to improve forward visibility for the pilot. The F4U-1A could also be fitted with a 170-gallon fuel tank under the fuselage, and Brewster developed a rack on which a

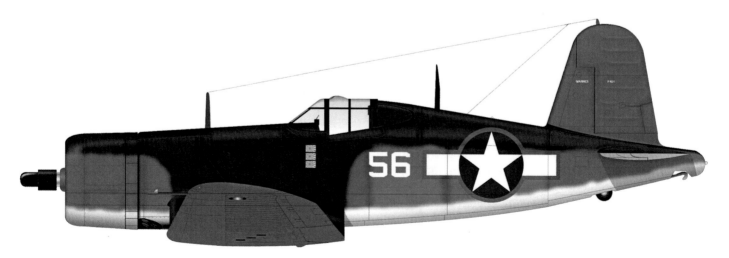

This F4U-1 was flown by Captain Harry Winfree while assigned to VMF-211 in the Solomon Islands in late 1943. The aircraft has the "birdcage" canopy and retains the red surround to the national insignia. Winfree was credited with three confirmed kills and four probables. (Artwork by Rock Roszak)

A semi-bubble canopy to improve visibility was a new feature on the F4U-1A. Brewster designed a special rack which could be fitted under the fuselage to carry a bomb. The Corsair proved to be a very effective fighter-bomber, and it was used extensively in this role in the Pacific theater. (National Archives)

bomb could be carried. Using this modification, the Corsair proved to be a very effective fighter-bomber. F4U-1A equivalents were produced by Goodyear as FG-1As and by Brewster as F3A-1As.

The F4U-1A was replaced on the production lines by two new versions which were built concurrently. The F4U-1C and F4U-1D were essentially the same except that the F4U-1C was armed with four 20-mm cannons, and the F4U-1D retained the six .50-caliber machine guns used in the previous Corsair variants. The 20-mm cannons were not as effective for aerial combat as the machine guns, because their rate and duration of fire was considerably less. By comparison, the F4U-1C's four 20-mm cannons had a total of 924 rounds of ammunition, while the six .50-caliber weapons in the F4U-1D were supplied with 2,400 rounds. However, the cannons were far more effective against ground targets, so F4U-1Cs were assigned to squadrons tasked primarily with providing close air support to Marines on the ground.

To further increase the fighter-bomber capabilities of the Corsair, both the F4U-1C and F4U-1D were fitted with two pylons under the center wing section that could carry bombs, napalm, or

154-gallon fuel tanks. During production of these two variants, rocket stubs were added under the outer wing panels to carry eight 5-inch High Velocity Aerial Rockets (HVAR).

Another change made during production was that the overhead frames of the canopy were deleted, and this further improved visibility. Another less important change was that the propeller was reduced in diameter from 13' 4" to 13' 1'.

Only two hundred F4U-1Cs were built, and they were built in small blocks in between larger production blocks of F4U-1Ds. All F4U-1Cs were built by Vought, but it was a different story for the F4U-1D. By this time, the Navy had become so displeased with the Brewster-built Corsairs that no F4U-1D equivalent was produced by Brewster. However, while Vought built 1,685 F4U-1Ds, Goodyear actually exceeded this total with the delivery of 1,997 FG-1Ds.

By the time the F4U-1D was entering service, the problems related to carrier suitability had been solved. The wing stall problem was corrected by adding a small spoiler to the leading edge of the right wing just outboard of the guns. This caused the two wings to

This F4U-1C of VMF-314 was the only Corsair in the squadron to have the unit's insignia painted on the fuselage. The squadron was called "Bob's Cats" after their squadron commander Bob Cameron. The insignia was a bobcat in boxing gloves charging forward with two lightning bolts. (Artwork by Rock Roszak)

The F4U-1C was essentially the same as the F4U-1D with the main difference being that the F4U-1C was armed with four 20-mm cannons instead of six .50-caliber machine guns as used in the F4U-1D. The powerful cannons were more potent when it came to attacking ground targets. When 5-inch rockets and bombs or napalm were added to the cannon armament, the F4U-1C was a truly formidable fighter-bomber. This F4U-1C was assigned to VMF-314 which operated from the island of Ie Shima during the invasion of Okinawa. Armorer John Shoulders poses with the well armed Corsair which is loaded with napalm and rockets for a mission on June 13, 1945. (Shoulders via Roszak)

Thirty-four F4U-2 night fighters were converted from existing F4U-1 airframes. An A1A radar antenna was installed inside a pod mounted on the leading edge of the right wing, and the radar scope was added at the center of the instrument panel. To balance the radar, the right outboard gun was deleted. These F4U-2s are assigned to VF(N)-101, and they are preparing to launch from USS ENTERPRISE, CV-6, for a raid against Truk. (USN via Jones)

stall at the same time, thus helping to keep the wings level during an approach to a carrier landing. By late 1944, more and more Corsairs were being assigned to squadrons aboard the large ESSEX class carriers, and some were even assigned to small escort carriers.

During World War II, the Royal Navy's Fleet Air Arm received a considerable number of Corsairs. Ninety-five F4U-1s were named Corsair Is by the British. The name Corsair II was given to 430 Brewster F3A-1s, and both F4U-1As and F4U-1Ds were called Corsair IIIs. FG-1Ds were named Corsair IVs. Unlike the U. S. Navy, the British started using their Corsairs aboard carriers from the beginning, believing that proper pilot training permitted the

powerful fighter to be operated safely aboard ships. All British Corsairs, except for the Corsair Is, had eight inches clipped from each wing tip so that they could fit in the hangar bays of British carriers with their wings folded. The only other nation to operate Corsairs during World War II was New Zealand, which received 424 Corsairs for the Royal New Zealand Air Force.

Even before the first F4U-1 made its maiden flight, the Navy had expressed an interest in a night fighter version of the Corsair. As a result, the first production F4U-1, BuNo. 02153, was modified to become the XF4U-2 prototype.

The conversion to a night fighter was accomplished by adding a pod which contained an A1A radar to the leading edge of the right wing. To help balance the weight of the radar, the outboard machine gun was removed from the right wing. The associated equipment for the radar was installed in the aft fuselage, and a

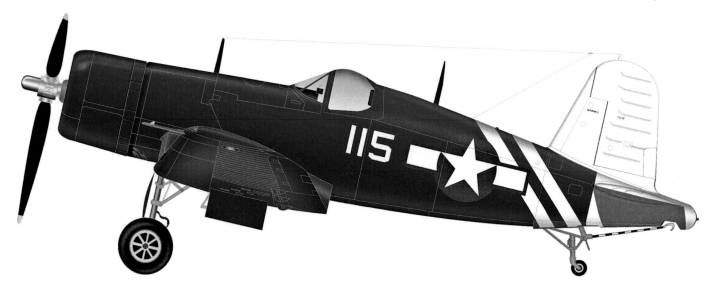

Large geometric markings adorn this Goodyear FG-1D assigned to VMF-213 aboard USS SAIDOR, CVE-117, during the late war period. Geometric markings, which became known as "G Markings," were specified for the Navy's fleet and light carrier-based aircraft in January 1945. But being assigned to an escort carrier, this Corsair has the markings assigned to the sixth ship in Carrier Division TWENTY-EIGHT in the CVE identification markings system put into place in June 1945. (Artwork by Rock Roszak)

An F4U-1D from VMF-224 is hooked up to the catapult aboard USS SIT-KOH BAY, CVE-86, on March 28, 1945. Note the holdback bar attached to the tail gear. This will break away when the catapult is fired. By the time the F4U-1D was produced, all of the Corsair's problems related to carrier suitability had been corrected. (NNAM)

small scope was added at the center of the instrument panel. Additionally, a radar altimeter and a radar beacon transponder were installed, and a VHF radio replaced the standard high frequency set. Thirty-two night fighters were converted from existing F4U-1s at the Naval Aircraft Factory, while two more were converted in the field. These thirty-four Corsairs were redesignated F4U-2s and were supplied to one Marine and two Navy night fighter squadrons.

In an attempt to develop a high altitude fighter, three XF4U-3 prototypes were converted from existing airframes. The first, designated the XF4U-3A, had an R-2800-16 engine installed, and the other two were fitted with an R-2800-14W. These were designated XF4U-3Bs All three had turbo-superchargers, but performance was only marginally better than the F4U-4 which was about to enter service. Goodyear upgraded thirteen FG-1Ds to XF4U-3B standards, but these were not used operationally.

In the final months of World War II, a new and considerably improved version of the Corsair was entering service. Designated the F4U-4, this variant could be distinguished by its four-blade propeller, but the changes were far more extensive than just having a different propeller. Powered by a R-2800-18W "C" series engine, the new Corsair had a maximum speed of 446 miles per hour. The cockpit was redesigned, and a floor was added. Only a few Marine squadrons saw combat with the F4U-4 before the war ended.

F4U-4s would remain in service for many years after the war, even when jet fighters became operational. F4U-4Bs were also produced, and these had four 20-mm cannons in place of the six .50-caliber machine guns. Many F4U-4s and F4U-4Bs saw service with Navy and Marine squadrons in Korea, as did later variants including the F4U-5 fighter-bomber, F4U-5N night fighter, F4U-5P photographic reconnaissance variant, and the AU-1 ground attack version.

Corsairs continued to roll off the production line until December 1952, the last ninety-four being delivered to the French Navy as F4U-7s. Production lasted for over a decade, and this was the longest production run for any U. S. fighter that fought in World War II. During the war, it scored a kill ratio of eleven to one over enemy aircraft, and it was also one of the most effective fighter-bomber and attack aircraft used by any nation.

Two F4U-1As were converted to XF4U-4Xs to begin development of the F4U-4 version of the Corsair. These were followed by five XF4U-4 prototypes. These aircraft, along with production F4U-4s, could be distinguished from earlier Corsair variants because of their four-blade propellers. (USN via Jones)

The last version of the Corsair to reach operational units during World War II was the F4U-4. Only a few saw service with Marine squadrons before the Japanese surrendered. These saw very little combat, but the F4U-4 would be used extensively in Korea. Initially, Pratt & Whitney R-2800-18W engines were installed in F4U-4s, but these were later replaced with R-2800-42Ws. The cockpit was redesigned, and a floor was added, replacing the two foot troughs used in earlier versions. This F4U-4 was assigned to VMF-225, and it is shown here shortly after the end of World War II. (NNAM)

F4U-1D & FG-1D COCKPIT DETAILS

Above: Although the elapsed time clock is missing from the top right corner, the instrument panel in the restored FG-1D at the National Naval Aviation Museum looks much as it did when the aircraft was operational. (Kinzey)

Up until the F4U-4 variant, Corsairs did not have cockpit floors. Instead, there were two troughs on which the pilot rested his feet. A rudder pedal was above each trough. (Kinzey)

As with most American fighters, the engine controls, fuel selector switch, bomb release lever, trim controls, and landing gear handle were on the left side of the cockpit. (Kinzey)

Many FG-1Ds were delivered with flat black cockpit sides, and this is one of them. The right console had switches for the electrical systems, radio controls, and the IFF control box. (Kinzey)

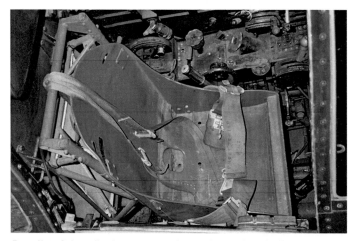

Details of the pilot's seat are shown here. Lap belts were usually considerably wider than the shoulder harnesses. All four belts were joined at a single point which had a quick release lever. (Kinzey)

A padded headrest was above the seat. Early F4U-1Ds and FG-1Ds had the same canopy as the F4U-1A which had two overhead frames, but most had this canopy that did not have the overhead frames. (Kinzey)

GRUMMAN F6F HELLCAT

The XF6F-1 was the initial prototype for the Hellcat line of fighters. It was powered by a Wright R-2600-10 engine with a Curtiss Electric propeller. The XF6F-1 could be distinguished from all other Hellcats by its L-shaped pitot probe on top of the right wing tip. (Grumman)

The XF6F-2 was to be evaluated with the Wright R-2600-15 fitted with a turbo-supercharger. However, this was changed to a Pratt & Whitney R-2800-21 which also had a turbo-supercharger installed in an attempt to provide more power at high altitudes. The scoop below the engine was enlarged to provide more air to the turbo-supercharger. The engine turned a large four-blade propeller, and a spinner was fitted to the hub. Evaluations with the XF6F-2 proved disappointing, and once the tests were complete, this Hellcat was brought up to F6F-3 standards and delivered to the Navy. (Grumman)

The primary mission of a fighter aircraft is to destroy enemy aircraft in order to establish control of the air. It must also be survivable so that it can continue to fight another day. If this is the yardstick by which a fighter is to be judged, then Grumman's F6F Hellcat is the most successful American fighter of all time. During World War II, U. S. Navy Hellcats shot down 5,156 enemy aircraft with a loss of only 270 F6Fs. This 19 to 1 kill ratio is the highest for any American fighter in the history of warfare when more than one hundred victories are considered. It is really not possible to say that any one fighter was the best in history or even at any point in time. There are too many variables, and what the fighter is designed to accomplish in a specific theater of operations must be clearly defined. Nevertheless, the remarkable record of the F6F Hellcat is undeniable, and it is certainly one of the most successful fighter designs of all time.

On June 30, 1941, the Navy placed an order with Grumman for two prototypes of a new single-engine fighter designated the XF6F-1 and XF6F-2. That same day a contract was also issued for three twin-engine XF7F-1s, so Grumman's design teams had their work cut out for them.

As a starting point, Grumman's engineers used the basic layout of the F4F Wildcat, which was replacing older fighters in Navy and Marine squadrons at that time. The XF6F-1 and XF6F-2 were in many respects a larger version of the Wildcat with a much more powerful engine. To relate the two aircraft, the new design was named the Hellcat, and what was to become a long line of Grumman "cat" fighters for the Navy was born. Although armament was not installed in the prototypes, the design called for six .50-caliber machine guns to be mounted in the wings.

An F6F-3 Hellcat is launched from the hangar deck catapult aboard USS HORNET, CV-12. Several of the early ESSEX class carriers had a catapult on their hanger decks, so aircraft could be launched while the flight deck was spotted for recovery operations with planes forward. However, the feature was deleted from later ESSEX class carriers. (NNAM)

The F6F-3N was the first night fighter version of the Hellcat that was built in considerable numbers, with approximately 200 being produced. It featured an AN/APS-6 radar that was housed in a pod near the right wing tip. The F6F-3E was also a night fighter version of the F6F-3, and it had an AN/APS-4 radar hung in a pod under the right wing. However, only eighteen F6F-3Es were built. (Grumman)

The XF6F-1 was powered by a supercharged Wright R-2600-10 engine capable of producing 1,600 horsepower. Original plans were for the XF6F-2 to be powered by a turbo-supercharged Wright R-2600-15, but this was changed to the turbo-supercharged Pratt & Whitney R-2800-21 instead. Results were less than favorable with the turbo-supercharger, so the XF6F-2 was later brought up to production F6F-3 standards and delivered to the Navy.

A third prototype, designated the XF6F-3, was ordered, and it was also fitted with a Pratt & Whitney R-2800-10, but in this aircraft, the engine was not turbo-supercharged. Instead, a standard supercharger was installed to increase performance at high altitudes. This became the standard for 4,402 production F6F-3s that were delivered to the Navy. The Royal Navy also received 252 F6F-3s which it called the Hellcat I.

The aircraft made its combat debut on August 31, 1943, when Hellcats from USS ESSEX, CV-9, USS YORKTOWN, CV-10, and USS INDEPENDENCE, CVL-22, attacked the Japanese at Mar-

Painted in the tri-color scheme, this F6F-3 was assigned to VF-1 aboard USS YORKTOWN, CV-10, during the "Marianas Turkey Shoot" in June 1944. VF-1's famous "Top Hat" insignia was painted on both sides of the fuselage beneath the windscreen. (Artwork by Rock Roszak)

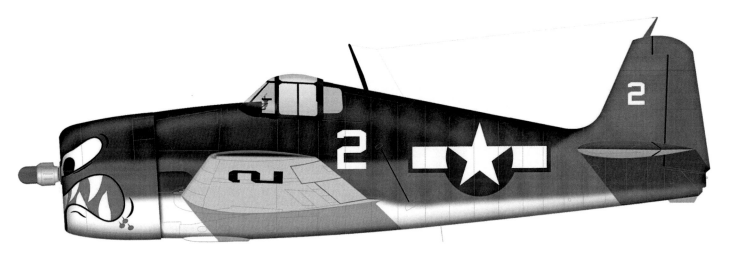

VF-27 flew both the F6F-3 and F6F-5 Hellcats, and featured some of the most garish unit markings displayed by U. S. Navy aircraft during the war. This "cat-mouthed" F6F-3 was aboard USS PRINCETON, CVL-23 in mid-1944. PRINCETON was lost on October 24, 1944 while operating in Leyte Gulf. (Artwork by Rock Roszak)

cus Island. From that date onward, more and more Hellcats joined the fleet as the war in the Pacific advanced steadily toward Japan.

Three sub-variants of the F6F-3 were converted from existing F6F-3 airframes. The F6F-3E was a night fighter fitted with a radar pod under its right wing. This housed an AN/APS-4 radar, and the associated equipment for the radar was housed in the aft fuselage. A radar scope and controls were located on the instrument panel in the cockpit. Only eighteen F6F-3Es were converted.

The more numerous and successful night fighter version of the F6F-3 was the F6F-3N. An AN/APS-6 radar was installed in a radome fixed to the leading edge of the right wing. A total of 205 F6F-3Ns were converted from existing F6F-3 deliveries, and these often worked in consort with TBF Avengers specially equipped for night fighting.

The third sub-variant of the F6F-3 was a photographic reconnaissance version fitted with cameras in the rear fuselage. Carriers would usually have three or four of these F6F-3Ps assigned to

their air wings to provide reconnaissance and post-strike photography to commanders.

Meanwhile, the XF6F-1 prototype was converted to the XF6F-4. This aircraft differed from the F6F-3 in two major respects. First, it was powered by a Pratt & Whitney R-2800-27 engine which produced 2,100 horsepower, and second, the six .50-caliber machine guns were replaced with four 20-mm cannons. This version was never put into production, and the aircraft was subsequently converted to F6F-3 standards and delivered to the Navy.

The major production variant of the Hellcat was the F6F-5; 6,681 of which were delivered. An additional 1,189 were produced as F6F-5N night fighters with the same AN/APS-6 radar in the pod on the right wing as on the F6F-3N. Some F6F-5s were converted to F6F-5P photo reconnaissance aircraft in essentially the same way as had been done with the previous F6F-3P. A total of 930 F6F-5s were delivered to the British who called them Hellcat IIs.

The major improvement on the F6F-5 was the ability to car-

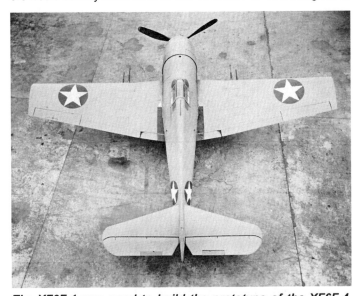

The XF6F-1 was used to build the prototype of the XF6F-4. This version replaced the six .50-caliber machine guns with four 20-mm cannons, and it was powered by a Pratt and Whitney R-2800-27 engine. However, this version of the Hellcat was never put into production, and the aircraft was converted to F6F-3 standards and delivered to the Navy. (Grumman)

The F6F-5 was the final production version of the Hellcat. It first flew in April 1944. This photograph of an F6F-5 was taken aboard USS SARATOGA, CV-3, on February 21, 1945, while the ship was under attack by the Japanese. Debris and smoke from a near bomb hit can be seen in the photo, and the wing of the Hellcat has been pierced by flying fragments. Note the carrier identification markings used by aircraft assigned to SARATOGA at that time. (U. S. Navy)

Ensign Thomas Tillar flew this F6F-5 from USS HORNET, CV-12, while he was assigned to VF-11 in September 1944. It was painted in the overall Gloss Sea Blue scheme. (Artwork by Rock Roszak)

The Hellcat night fighter variant that was produced in the largest numbers was the F6F-5N, which housed an AN/APS-6 radar in a pod near the right wing tip. This F6F-5N was assigned to Marine squadron VMF-511, and it is shown operating aboard the second USS BLOCK IS-LAND, CVE-106, in February 1945. (U. S. Navy)

A few F6F-3s and F6F-5s were converted for photographic reconnaissance work and re-designated F6F-3P and F6F-5P respectively. This was accomplished simply by adding cameras in the aft fuselage and providing controls to operate them in the cockpit. Each carrier usually had several of these photo-Hellcats aboard. These two F6F-5Ps were assigned to VF-85 aboard USS SHANGRI-LA, CV-38, and they display that carrier's Z code on their vertical tails. This photo is dated August 17, 1945. (U. S. Navy)

Hellcats even operated from some of the escort carriers, including the four of the SANGAMON class. Here an F6F-5 launches from USS SUWANEE, CVE-27, on August 30, 1945. (U. S. Navy)

ry external ordnance. Two 500 or 1,000-pound bombs could be carried on pylons under the wings between the landing gear, and the centerline station remained to carry an external fuel tank. Six 5-inch rockets could be carried on stubs under the folding outboard wing sections. David McCampbell, the Navy's leading ace, told the author, Bert Kinzey, in an interview that he often carried rockets on his F6F-5 and used them in aerial combat.

Like the F6F-3, early F6F-5s had the window on each side of the fuselage just aft of the cockpit, but this feature was deleted early in the production run. The windscreen was redesigned as was the cowling, but otherwise there was little change between the F6F-3 and F6F-5. The easiest way to distinguish between the two major Hellcat variants was to look at the paint scheme. F6F-5s were all delivered in the overall Gloss Sea Blue scheme. A few early F6F-3s were completed in the Blue-Gray over Light Gray scheme, but most F6F-3s were delivered in the tri-color scheme.

Two XF6F-6 prototypes were built, and these had the more powerful Pratt & Whitney R-2800-18W "C" engine with a four-blade propeller. This increased horsepower to 2,450, and performance improved significantly. However, the war ended before any production F6F-6s were built.

In the post-war years, Hellcats were replaced in operational squadrons by later variants of the F4U Corsair and the F8F Bearcat. But Hellcats continued to serve in training squadrons and with the Naval Reserve for several years.

Grumman proposed a final production version of the Hellcat, and two XF6F-6 prototypes were built using existing airframes 70188 and 70913. The XF6F-6 first flew on July 6, 1944, and it achieved a top speed of 417 miles per hour. It featured a very tight fitting cowling to streamline the aircraft, and it was powered by a Pratt & Whitney R2800-18W engine that turned a four-blade Hamilton Standard propeller. However, this version of the Hellcat was never ordered by the Navy. (Grumman)

F6F-3 COCKPIT DETAILS

Hellcats had a very simple cockpit with basic flight instruments and controls all within easy reach of the pilot. The photos on this page were taken in the F6F-3 on display at the National Naval Aviation Museum. (Kinzey)

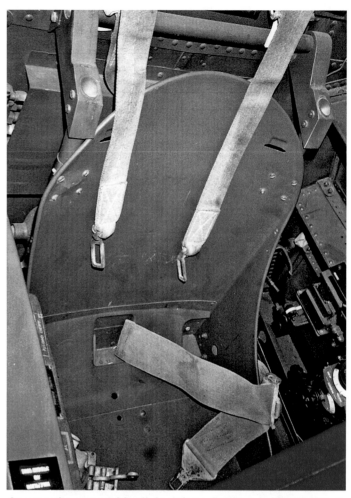

As was the case with all American fighters in World War II, Hellcats had an all-metal seat for the pilot. Lap belts and shoulder harnesses kept the pilot secure in the seat during flight. The parachute pack fit into the bucket and served as the seat cushion. (Kinzey)

The throttle quadrant, fuel selector, trim controls, flap controls, and the landing gear lever were all located on the left side of the cockpit. Check lists for take-off and landing were printed on a small placard on the cockpit rail. (Kinzey)

The electrical distribution panel, circuit breakers, controls for the oxygen system, and the radio controls were on the right side of the cockpit. The Identification Friend or Foe (IFF) control box was behind the coiled cord for the hand microphone. (Kinzey)

VOUGHT XF5U-1 FLYING PANCAKE

The V-173, BuNo. 02978, was the flying prototype for the XF5U-1, and it was used to test the concept of a flying disc before development of the XF5U-1. (NNAM)

In 1938, a NACA aeronautical engineer named Charles H. Zimmerman theorized that an airfoil in the form of a disc would offer incredible performance not possible with a conventional wing design. Using scale models, Zimmerman tested his theories and claimed that, using large propellers, he could make a circular airfoil take off and land in a very short distance, practically hover in the air, yet fly at speeds in excess of five-hundred miles-per-hour.

The following year, Zimmerman was hired by Vought, and he designed a full scale flying prototype employing the design characteristics he had developed with his models. Called the V-173, the prototype was intended only to prove the concepts before full scale developmental aircraft were built. It was constructed of wood and fabric and powered by two 80-horsepower Continental A-80 engines that turned huge wooden propellers that were 16 feet, 6 inches in diameter.

The first flight of this aircraft was made on November 23, 1942, and although underpowered, the V-173 took off and landed in only fifty feet. The aircraft was stall proof, and no matter how tightly it was turned, it did not fall off into a stall.

Convinced that the circular airfoil had merit, the Navy proceeded with development of two fighter prototypes designated XF5U-1. One was to be used for static testing, while the other would be used for flight tests. These were to be powered by two Pratt & Whitney R-2000-7 engines turning four-blade articulated propellers which functioned like the main rotor of a helicopter. Projected top speed was 460 miles-per-hour, while landing speed was only twenty miles-per-hour. The cockpit was fitted with an ejection seat, and unofficially the aircraft became known as the "Flying Pancake," but the monikers "Flying Flapjack" and "Saucer" were also used.

Although the first prototype was ready for testing in August 1945, the revolutionary articulated propellers were not available until 1947. In late 1948, flight testing still had not begun, and the static prototype had been scrapped. By then the Navy had made a commitment to jet power for all of its future fighters, so the flying prototype of the XF5U-1 was also scrapped without ever being flown.

A front view of the XF5U-1 shows the circular inlets for the engines and the large four-blade articulated propellers which operated much like the rotor blades of a helicopter. (NNAM)

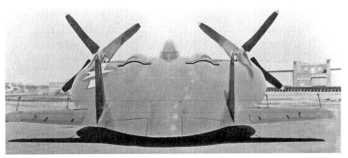

Ailevators, which performed the functions of both ailerons for roll control and elevators for pitch control, are visible in this rear view. Flaps were located at the aft end of the fuselage between the vertical tails. (NNAM)

GRUMMAN F7F TIGERCAT

The first XF7F-1 prototype was unpainted and had TEST lettered on both sides of the nose in yellow with a black outline. Note the large spinners on the propeller hubs. (NNAM)

June 30, 1941, was a significant day in the history of the Grumman Aircraft Engineering Corporation. On that date, it received not one but two contracts to build prototypes of fighter aircraft. One was for the XF6F-1 Hellcat, which was to become the most numerous and successful U. S. Navy fighter in World War II. The second was for the XF7F-1 Tigercat, a large twin-engine design based on lessons learned with the XF5F-1 Skyrocket. Although it would not be produced in anywhere near the same numbers nor earn the acclaim and success of the Hellcat, the Tigercat did introduce a new class of fighters to the Navy. It was the first twin-engine carrier-based fighter designed for the Navy to become operational, and it was also the first operational shipboard fighter to have a tricycle landing gear. However, as things would work out, it was never considered acceptable for carrier operations, and its use aboard carriers was very limited to the point of being almost non-existent.

Designed to operate from the new MIDWAY class of large aircraft carriers then under construction, the Tigercat was intended to be a heavily armed, long range fighter-bomber. Internal armament consisted of four .50-caliber machine guns in the nose and four 20-mm cannons in the wing roots. Two 1,000-pound bombs could be carried on hardpoints under the wings, and a 2,000-pound torpedo could be carried beneath the fuselage.

The first of two XF7F-1 prototypes made its maiden flight on December 2, 1943, with Grumman test pilot Robert Hall at the controls. It was powered by two Pratt & Whitney R-2800-22W engines, each of which produced 2,100 horsepower. Large spinners were mounted to the propeller hubs, and although these initially remained on early production F7F-1s, they were soon eliminated.

The first XF7F-1 prototype crashed on May 1, 1944, but the test program was continued by the second prototype. Early production F7F-1s soon joined the program including conducting carrier trials aboard USS SHANGRI-LA, CV-38, in November. Although the performance and capabilities of the aircraft were quite impressive, the large fighter was deemed unsuitable for carrier operations.

The Marine Corps received the first Tigercats to be delivered to operational squadrons. The tremendous firepower was exactly what the Marines needed as they fought against the Japanese on

F7F-1, BuNo. 80291, was used for carrier suitability trials aboard USS SHANGRI-LA, CV-38. The trials were flown on November 15, 1944, by Marine pilot C. S. Lane, who was assigned to HEDRON MAG-91. The Tigercat was originally designed as a fighter-bomber that would operate from the larger MIDWAY class carriers then under construction, but carrier evaluations were not deemed to be satisfactory. As a result, Tigercats operated almost exclusively from land bases throughout their service life. Later carrier trials conducted by VMF-534 with F7F-3Ns also proved unsatisfactory. (NNAM)

The F7F-2N was the first two-seat night fighter version of the Tigercat. It was equipped with an AN/APS-6 radar in the nose, and this meant that the four .50-caliber machine guns had to be removed, leaving the four 20-mm cannons in the wing roots as the internal armament. Launchers for eight 5-inch rockets were added under the outer wing panels. One of the fuel cells in the fuselage had to be removed to make room for a second cockpit for the radar operator. This F7F-2N is shown at the Naval Air Test Center at NAS Patuxent River, Maryland, during the post-war years. (Grumman)

islands across the Pacific, but the war ended before the Tigercats saw any combat.

Although 500 F7F-1s had been included in the initial order for Tigercats, production of this version was terminated after only thirty-four had been completed. Production then changed to a two-seat night fighter version designated F7F-2N. One XF7F-2N prototype and sixty-four production aircraft were delivered. The four .50-caliber machine guns in the nose were deleted to allow for the installation of an AN/APS-6 search radar, thus leaving the four 20-mm cannons as internal armament, and the internal fuel capacity was reduced to make room for a second cockpit for the radar operator. Eight launchers for 5-inch rockets were installed under the outer wing panels.

Many people think of a night fighter's role as being only for air-to-air combat, but this was not the case for the night fighter versions of the Tigercat. Their radars could identify surface targets, and effective interdiction attacks could be made against them in the darkness of night. Many of the F7F-2Ns were converted to

F7F-2D drone controllers. The second cockpit was raised and covered with the windscreen and canopy like that used on the F8F Bearcat.

By March 1945, the new single-seat F7F-3 day fighters were coming off the production line. These were essentially the same as the original single-place F7F-1s except that they had the more powerful R-2800-34W engines, each of which provided 250 more horsepower than the R-2800-22W used in the F7F-1. Early F7F-3s had the same vertical tail as the previous variants, but starting with BuNo. 80365, the area of the vertical tail was increased to improve directional stability. This day fighter had the four .50-caliber machine guns in the nose like the F7F-1, and 189 were produced. With the war coming to an end, orders for an additional 1,389 were cancelled. Sixty-one F7F-3s were converted to F7F-3P long range photographic-reconnaissance aircraft which had oblique and vertical cameras installed in the aft fuselage.

In 1946, sixty F7F-3N two-seat night fighters were delivered, and like the earlier F7F-2N, the F7F-3N had a second cockpit for the radar operator, but its nose was redesigned to house the SCR-720 search radar. This modification meant that the four .50-caliber machine guns had to be deleted as they had been in the F7F-2N. In the early stages of the Korean War, F7F-3Ns assigned to VMF(N)-513 and based at Kimpo Air Base shot down two Polikar-

The second single-seat version of the Tigercat to go into production was the F7F-3. Only 189 were produced, while orders for 1,389 were canceled as World War II came to an end. BuNo. 80405 is seen here as it appeared in mid-1945. Note the larger vertical tail that was added during F7F-3 production. The bands on the fuselage, wings, and cowlings were medium green with white borders. This aircraft was assigned to HEDRON 1, a U. S. Marine Corps squadron. (NNAM)

Some F7F-2Ns were converted to F7F-2D drone controllers. The raised cockpit for the controller was covered by an F8F Bearcat canopy, and an ADF antenna was located on top of the nose. Colorful yellow and red markings were applied to the aircraft which were flown by utility squadrons. (NNAM)

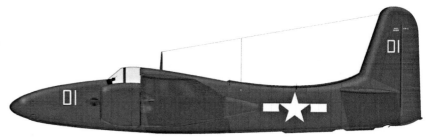

F7F-3P, BuNo 80359, was flown by Major U. O. Ullman when he was the commanding officer of VMD-254 in April 1945. This particular Tigercat had originally been completed as the first F7F-3, but it was converted to an F7F-3P. (Artwork by Rock Roszak)

F7F-3Ps of VMD-2 (previously designated VMD-954 until March 25, 1945) are pictured on Okinawa in September 1945. The squadron arrived in theater on the day the war ended, and they would remain there into 1946 doing photo-reconnaissance work to monitor Japan's compliance with treaty requirements. (NNAM)

The F7F-3N could be identified by its modified nose with the fairing below it. This housed an SCR-720 radar. This particular F7F-3N was used by Grumman to test carrying external stores. For this flight, a Mk 13 aerial torpedo has been attached beneath the fuselage. Mk 9 rocket launchers can be seen beneath the wing. (Grumman)

pov Po-2 biplanes, marking the only use of the Tigercat in combat. These F7F-3Ns soon became victims of the jet age and were replaced with F3D Skyknights.

The final version of the Tigercat was the F7F-4N, but only one prototype and twelve production aircraft were built. All were two-seat night fighters, and they had an AN/APS-19 search radar mounted in the nose. Unlike the previous F7F-3N, the nose did not have to be redesigned to house this type of radar.

The F7F-4N had strengthened wings after carrier trials with the F7F-3N had demonstrated that the wings were not strong enough for repeated carrier landings. Nevertheless, the F7F-4N, like all previous variants, operated almost exclusively from land

The pilot of an F7F-3N assigned to VMF(N)-513 starts his engines at Kunsan Air Base Korea. During the early part of the Korean War, F7F-3Ns from this squadron shot down two Polikarpov Po-2 biplanes, marking the only use of the Tigercat in combat. The F7F-3Ns were soon replaced with F3D Skyknight night fighters that were powered by two jet engines. (U. S. Navy)

An F7F-3N launches from USS TARAWA, CV-40, off the coast of Hawaii in 1946. As was the case with the early F7F-1, these carrier evaluations with the F7F-3N indicated that the Tigercat was not well suited for carrier operations. (U. S. Navy)

bases, and far more Tigercats served with the Marines than with the Navy. The only occasions any Tigercats operated from aircraft carriers were for very short trials and evaluation periods, and the aircraft was never considered suitable for sustained shipboard deployments.

Although the Tigercat never served in its intended role as a carrier-based fighter-bomber, it remained operational for almost a decade, serving primarily as a long-range night fighter. It will always have a place in the history of military aviation as the only twin-engine propeller-driven fighter ever to enter operational service with the U. S. Navy and Marine Corps.

Details in the front cockpit of an F7F-3N night fighter are revealed in this photograph. The interior was painted black. (Grumman)

One of the twelve production F7F-4Ns flies out of its home base of Naval Air Station, Key West, Florida. The aircraft was assigned to FCN-2, and this photograph was taken in February 1948. Unlike the previous F7F-3N, the F7F-4N had an AN/APS-19 search radar fitted in a standard nose section. (NNAM)

CURTISS XF14C

After plans to fit the XF14C-1 with a Lycoming XH-2470-4 fell through due to delays with the powerplant, the aircraft was completed as the XF14C-2. It had a Wright XR-3350-16 radial engine turning two contra-rotating propellers. (NNAM)

On June 30, 1941, the Navy issued three contracts for the development of new fighters. Two went to Grumman for the XF6F-1 Hellcat and XF7F-1 Tigercat, while the third went to Curtiss for the XF14C.

Designed as a high-altitude fighter, the XF14C-1 was to be powered by a Lycoming XH-2470-4 Hyper engine producing 2,200 horsepower at sea level. The use of this liquid-cooled powerplant was a marked departure from the Navy's long-standing insistence of using air-cooled, radial engines on its aircraft. The engine had twenty-four cylinders in four rows of six each that were mounted in an H configuration, hence the H in the powerplant's designation.

Initial wind tunnel tests in October 1942 indicated that top speed would be well below the Curtiss estimates. Adding to this problem, the Lycoming powerplant experienced problems which caused unacceptable delays, and as a result the XF14C-1 project was canceled. Instead, a turbo-supercharged Wright XR-3350-16 Duplex Cyclone air-cooled engine that produced 2,300 horsepower was substituted, and the aircraft was redesignated the XF14C-2. In an attempt to improve high-altitude performance, the engine turned two contra-rotating propellers.

Although the initial contract called for the aircraft to be armed with four or six .50-caliber machine guns, the Navy, in another departure from the norm, later changed the armament to four 20-mm cannons. At that time, almost all U. S. fighter aircraft were armed with machine guns, with .50-caliber weapons being used predominantly throughout the war years in both Army and Navy fighters. The few exceptions where 20-mm cannons were used on specialized sub-variants of existing fighter designs that like the F4U-1C Corsair. The four 20-mm cannons had barrels that extended well forward of the leading edge of the wings, and they were covered by long tapered fairings.

After many delays, the first flight of the one XF14C-2 prototype took place in July 1944, and although the aircraft climbed to 39,500 feet, the top speed of 418 miles-per-hour was well below expectations. There were also vibration problems caused by the powerplant and contra-rotating propellers, and these were never solved.

An XF14C-3, which featured a pressurized cockpit for high-altitude operations, was proposed, and the Navy originally planned to have Curtiss produce two prototypes of this design. However, before a contract was formalized, the entire XF14C project was canceled.

A left front view provides a better look at the two contra-rotating propellers and the four 20-mm cannons mounted in the wings. The exhaust for the turbo-supercharger can be seen under the fuselage. (NNAM)

GRUMMAN F8F BEARCAT

The first XF8F-1 flies a test flight over Long Island, New York, near Grumman's Bethpage plant. TEST is lettered in yellow on both sides of the fuselage. (Grumman)

The concept of mating a powerful engine to the lightest possible airframe led to the development of the Grumman F8F Bearcat. The Navy wanted a fighter with outstanding performance that could operate from even the smallest escort carriers. Intended primarily to be an interceptor, the new fighter would climb quickly to meet Japanese aircraft, particularly the Kamikazes, that were attacking the fleet. Accordingly, speed, rate-of-climb, and maneuverability were more important than range or the ability to carry heavy loads of external ordnance.

Grumman received a contract to build two XF8F-1 prototypes on November 27, 1943. Work progressed rapidly, and the first of the prototypes flew only ten months later on August 21, 1944. The second prototype followed in November, and deliveries began the following month.

The prototypes were powered by a Pratt & Whitney R-2800-22W engine which delivered 2,100 horsepower. Internal armament consisted of four .50-caliber machine guns mounted in the wings, and two 1,000-pound bombs or fuel tanks could be carried under the wings. Later F8F-1s could also carry four 5-inch rockets.

The Bearcat was a full twenty percent lighter than the F6F Hellcat which used the same engine. Accordingly, flight testing showed impressive performance. A novel feature was that the wing tips were designed to break away if the pilot over-stressed the aircraft during maneuvers. Explosive charges would blow off the opposite wing tip to provide balanced lift while maintaining control with the ailerons. This feature was later deleted from production Bearcats.

At the Joint Fighter Conference of 1944, the F8F-1 was flown in mock combat against the best American fighters of the day including the P-47D and P-47M Thunderbolt, P-51D Mustang, and the F4U-4 Corsair. The Army, Navy, and contractor pilots who flew the aircraft overwhelmingly voted it the best fighter in air-to-air combat below 25,000 feet. While the Mustang was better at higher altitudes, at altitudes where most aerial combat took place, the Bearcat was clearly superior.

Before the end of the war, Grumman had orders for 2,023 F8F-1s, and the Eastern Aircraft Division of General Motors had another order for 1,876 identical aircraft designated F3M-1s. But these orders were among the many that suffered deep cuts with

This F8F-1 was assigned to VF-19 when that squadron flew its carrier qualifications aboard USS RANGER, CV-4, in May 1945. (Artwork by Rock Roszak)

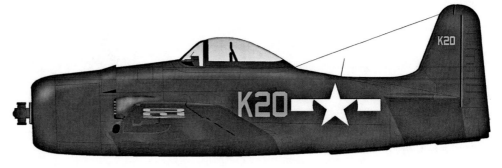

Deck crewmen stand by to pull the chocks from F8F-1s in preparation for launching from USS TARAWA, CV-40, in 1948. Aircraft 106 was assigned to VF-15A. (NNAM)

the end of the war in September 1945. The contract with Eastern was cancelled in its entirety, and Grumman's production line delivered only 765 F8F-1s. These were generally the same as the second XF8F-1, except that the R-2800-22W engine was replaced with the R-2800-34W during the production run.

VF-19 was the first squadron to transition to the F8F-1, and other squadrons began to receive Bearcats during the summer of 1945. However, none of these saw any combat before the war ended.

Although the Navy knew that future fighters would be powered by turbojet engines, it still needed the best possible propeller-driven fighter until the new jets could be developed and then become operational with the fleet squadrons. Many questions had to be answered before this could take place, because it appeared that jet aircraft might not be compatible with carrier operations. Eventually, the problems of adapting jets to carrier operations would be solved, but until they were, Bearcat production continued.

In 1946, the Navy formed the Blue Angels flight demonstration team, and the F6F-5 Hellcat was initially selected as the team's first aircraft. Additionally, an SNJ-6 trainer, which was painted yellow, flew as a Japanese "Zero," and the team engaged it in mock combat during their shows. But in August 1946, after only ten public appearances with the Hellcat, the Blue Angels flew to Grumman's plant in Bethpage, New York, where they put on a private show for Grumman's employees. After the show, they exchanged their F6F-5 Hellcats for F8F-1 Bearcats. The Bearcats were painted solid blue with yellow markings and numbered 1 through 4, just as the Hellcats had been. The Blue Angels also retained the SNJ-6 to continue the mock combat feature of their shows. In 1947, another Bearcat was added to the team. This was given the number 5, and it became the first solo aircraft with the Blues. In 1949, the SNJ-6 was replaced with a sixth Bearcat, but unlike the other 5, it was painted yellow and numbered 0, just as the SNJ-6 had been. However, rather than having Japanese Hinamarus,

The Blue Angels began flying F8F-1 Bearcats in 1946, and the yellow Beetle Bomb was added to the team in 1949. Although the Blues would transition to the F9F-2 Panther in late August of that year, the yellow Bearcat would remain with the team through the 1952 season. It is shown here with Bearcats 1 through 4 at a show at the Naval Air Facility in Salem, Oregon, on August 5, 1949. (NNAM)

An F8F-1B assigned to VF-12 flies near NAS Jacksonville, Florida, in 1949. (NNAM)

it had the same markings as the other Bearcats assigned to the team, only they were in Sea Blue. The SNJ-6 had been named "Beetle Bomb" in its last year of service with the team, and this name was carried forward to the new yellow Bearcat. Although the Blue Angels transitioned to the F9F-2 Panther as its show aircraft in August 1949, the yellow Bearcat remained with the team through 1952.

Meanwhile, the next production version of the Bearcat had entered the fleet. The F8F-1B differed from the original F8F-1 only in that it was armed with four 20-mm cannons instead of four .50-caliber machine guns. A total of 126 F8F-1Bs were delivered. Several of the original order were modified to carry a pod containing an AN/APS-19 radar under the right wing. A scope and radar controls were added in the cockpit. Records vary as to exactly how many Bearcats were converted to the night fighter F8F-1N configuration, but the number appears to have been no more than fifteen.

Production of a new version of the Bearcat began in 1948. Designated the F8F-2, it was powered by an R-2800-30W engine which increased maximum horsepower to 2,250. It also featured Automatic Engine Control (AEC) which combined the throttle and variable speed supercharger in one control. The increased torque of the -30W engine meant that the more rudder control was necessary to counter it, so the height of the vertical tail and rudder was increased by twelve inches. Grumman produced 293 F8F-2s and sixty F8F-2P photographic reconnaissance aircraft. The F8F-2Ps carried cameras in the aft fuselage, and armament was reduced to only two 20-mm cannons. Twelve F8F-2N night fighters were

An F8F-1B is attached to a land-based catapult for evaluations. Note the cannon barrels extending forward of the leading edge of the wings. (Grumman)

F8F-1, BuNo. 95049, was one of two F8F-1s converted for use as XF8F-2 prototypes. It is seen here at the Naval Air Test Center at NAS Patuxent River, Maryland, with the Pratt & Whitney R2800-30W engine installed, but without the addition of the taller vertical tail and four 20-mm cannons. The other XF8F-2 prototype was converted from F8F-1, BuNo. 95330. (NNAM)

An F8F-2 from VF-194 is brought up to the flight deck on the port side elevator aboard USS BOXER, CV-21. In addition to the taller vertical tail, another identifying feature of the later Bearcats was that the F8F-2 only had three exhaust stubs in the recessed area on each side of the fuselage, rather than the five on each side as seen on the F8F-1 and F8F-1B. (NNAM)

also built, and these carried the same AN/APS-19 radar used in the F8F-1N.

The Bearcat had been replaced by jet fighters by the time the Korean War began, but a few saw combat in Southeast Asia with the French and the Vietnamese. Others were also provided to the Royal Thai Air Force. Because the F8F served for such a relatively short period of time, and because it was a lightweight aircraft with a powerful engine, surplus Bearcats became a favorite of racing pilots, and many became air racers in the 1950s and beyond. Some were extensively modified and streamlined for this purpose.

The F8F Bearcat remains the last fighter to enter service with the U. S. Navy and Marines that was powered solely by a piston engine. Late versions of the F4U remained in service after the Bearcat had been retired, but the Corsair had entered service prior to the Bearcat.

Displaying its taller vertical tail and rudder, an F8F-2 assigned to VF-62 is ready to be launched from the starboard catapult aboard USS CORAL SEA, CVB-43. (NNAM)

Two F8F-2Ps fly above their carrier, USS ORISKANY, CV-34. Sixty of the photo-reconnaissance version of the Bearcat were produced, and the cameras were carried in the lower fuselage, just aft of the wings. The F8F-2P only had one 20-mm cannon in each wing, rather than the two on standard F8F-2s. (NNAM)

F8F-2 COCKPIT DETAILS

A surviving F8F-2 is on display at the National Naval Aviation Museum at NAS Pensacola, Florida. The cockpit remains as it was when the aircraft was in service. A reflector gunsight was mounted above the instrument panel. (Kinzey)

Ten basic flying instruments were situated on the main instrument panel, while engine and system instruments were located on the center pedestal. The control column was painted in the Grumman Bronze Green interior color. (Kinzey)

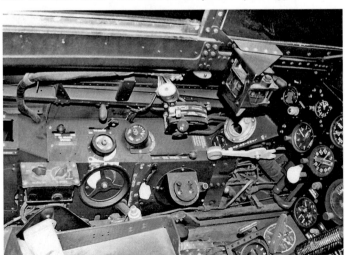

The engine and propeller controls were located on the quadrant above the left console. Trim wheels and the landing gear lever were among the items on the left side of the cockpit. (Kinzey)

Switches for the electrical systems were located on the right side of the cockpit along with the oxygen supply and the canopy control lever. The handle next to the seat was the emergency hydraulic hand pump. (Kinzey)

BOEING XF8B-1

Boeing's huge XF8B-1 was developed as a long-range heavy fighter-bomber, but it really belonged in the class of attack aircraft that subsequently materialized in the form of the Douglas AD Skyraider. (NNAM)

By 1943, the Navy was looking ahead to a possible invasion of the Japanese home islands. A long-range aircraft, capable of escorting bombers and carrying a significant weapons load of its own, was needed, and on May 4, 1943, Boeing received a contract for three prototypes to be designated XF8B-1.

As designed, the new fighter-bomber was powered by a 3,000-horsepower Pratt & Whitney XR-4360-10 Wasp Major engine turning two contra-rotating propellers. Internal armament was to be six .50-caliber machine guns or six 20-mm cannons.

An internal weapons bay could carry two 1,600-pound bombs, and two more bombs of the same size could be carried under the wings. Alternatively, two 2,000-pound torpedoes could be carried on the underwing stations.

The first prototype XF8B-1 made its initial flight on November 27, 1944, and performance was outstanding. But by the time the second and third prototypes joined the test program, the war was coming to an end, and no production orders were placed.

As the war ended, the Navy realized that future fighters would be jet powered, but the lessons learned in the development of the XF8B-1, and other similar prototypes then under development, were not forgotten by the Navy. They would lead to the attack type of aircraft, and this would result in the development of the Douglas AD Skyraider.

Left: The cockpit layout in the XF8B-1 was very similar to other American fighter aircraft of World War II. Additional instruments, used for test and evaluation flights, were attached to the coaming above the instrument panel. (NNAM)

Above: A rear view shows the large flaps on the XF8B-1 in the extended position. The large aircraft could carry up to 6,200 pounds of bombs or torpedoes in its internal weapons bay and under its wings. It was truly a multi-role aircraft that could serve as a long-range fighter, scout/dive bomber, or torpedo bomber. Although the XF8B-1 offered impressive performance, the Navy cancelled the program in favor of developing new jet fighters. (NNAM)

RYAN FR-1 FIREBALL

With his radial engine shut down and his propeller feathered, the pilot of this FR-1 cruises on jet power alone. When the Fireball was operational, pilots enjoyed flying up next to other aircraft with both engines running. They would then shut down the radial engine and feather the propeller. Since the FR-1 was not a well-known aircraft, the pilots and crewmen in the other aircraft looked on in astonishment as the Fireball continued to fly on and even accelerate away seemingly without its engine running. (NNAM)

During World War II, the development of gas turbine engines moved forward at a rapid pace. Germany led the way with the Me 262, which became the first operational jet fighter, and Great Britain followed closely behind with the Gloster Meteor. America lagged further back, but work was underway on several jet fighter designs as the war neared its conclusion. These included the Bell XP-59 and the Lockheed XP-80.

Although the turbojet engine offered the promise of higher speeds and overall greater performance, it also had severe limitations. Among these were slow acceleration, long take-off and landing rolls, high approach speeds, and very limited endurance. Carrier operations required takeoffs and landings in very short

distances, and flights over great expanses of water necessitated good endurance, not only to meet combat requirements, but for safety considerations as well. While catapults and arresting gear would help solve the take-off and landing problems, the Navy believed that the early jet engines failed to provide the quick power responses needed for shipboard operations.

Because of this, the Navy wanted to take a very conservative approach as jet engines were introduced to shipboard aircraft. They opted for a composite fighter with both a standard radial engine and a small jet powerplant located inside the fuselage. They insisted that the basic design of the airframe and airfoil remain as close to existing and proven standards for carrier aircraft as pos-

VF-66 conducted successful carrier evaluations with three FR-1s aboard USS RANGER, CV-4, in May 1945. (NNAM)

The wings are folded on B7 as it is moved between the flight deck and the hangar deck aboard RANGER. (NNAM)

This rear view photograph of an FR-1, taken at NAS Patuxent River, Maryland, in March 1945, provides a good look at the tail section of the aircraft including the exhaust pipe for the jet engine. (U. S. Navy)

sible. This was to insure that the aircraft handled well at the slow speeds necessary for carrier approaches and landings.

Nine aircraft manufacturers submitted proposals for a composite fighter in late 1942. Among these was a design submitted by the Ryan Company, best known for designing and building Charles Lindberg's Spirit of St. Louis. In spite of the fact that Ryan had never built a combat aircraft, much less one intended to operate from aircraft carriers, they were selected to proceed with the development and production of three prototypes. A contract was issued on February 11, 1943, and work began immediately on the three XFR-1s.

In most respects, the design was much like that of other radial engine fighters then under development. An unusual feature was that the aircraft had a tricycle landing gear, so the exhaust of the jet engine would not scorch and burn the wooden flight decks on aircraft carriers. The main gear retracted outward into wells under the wing rather than in the more conventional inward direction. The wings were mounted low on the fuselage, and the horizontal tail was mounted high on the fuselage beneath the vertical tail. In flight, the XFR-1 could easily be mistaken for an F8F Bearcat. A Wright R-1820-72W radial engine, which developed 1,350 horsepower, provided good low altitude and low speed performance. A small GE J31 jet engine was installed in the fuselage. Although it produced only 1,600 pounds of thrust, it was enough for the aircraft to fly on alone. The pilot could fully feather the propeller and cruise on jet power, or he could fly on just the radial engine. But in

most cases, both engines were running when the Fireball was in the air.

A contract was issued for one hundred production FR-1s on December 2, 1943, even before the first prototype was ready to fly. That flight took place on June 25, 1944, and a second order for an additional 600 FR-1s was placed on January 31, 1945, the same month initial deliveries of the first production FR-1s began reaching the Navy.

VF-66 was formed at NAS San Diego specifically to become operational with the new composite fighter. They began receiving their aircraft in March 1945, and in May they conducted carrier qualifications with three FR-1s aboard USS RANGER, CV-4. This squadron was later reformed as VF-41, and later this designation was changed to VF-1E.

The war ended before VF-66 could be deployed to the combat area, and with the end of the war, production of the FR-1 was terminated after only sixty-six aircraft had been completed. In the years following the war, the reformed VF-41 and VF-1E conducted carrier operations from several escort carriers including USS WAKE ISLAND, CVE-65, USS BAIROKO, CVE-115, and USS BADOENG STRAIT, CVE-116. The Fireball always operated with ease, even aboard the small carriers, but they were withdrawn from service in late 1947. By that time, advancements with turbojet engines and aircraft design had solved many of the problems related to carrier operations, and the Navy was fully committed to developing jet fighters for its carrier air groups.

Standard markings for VF-66 consisted only of a yellow B followed by the aircraft's number on the fuselage. The number was also repeated on the cowl ring and the vertical tail. (Artwork by Rock Roszak)

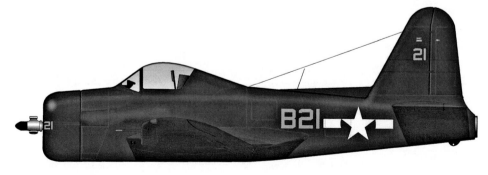

When this photo was taken, the squadron commander's aircraft for VF-66 was coded B1, and it had two yellow stripes around the aft fuselage. The vertical and horizontal tail surfaces, along with the aft fuselage, were painted white. (NNAM)

An FR-1 from VF-1E takes off from the escort carrier, USS BA-DOENG STRAIT, CVE-116, without the aid of a catapult. The squadron had formerly been designated VF-41. The red stripe had been added to the national insignia when this photo was taken in 1947. (NNAM)

Center Left: In addition to the four internal .50-caliber machine guns, the Fireball could carry a modest amount of external stores. In this view, an FR-1 carries four 5-inch rockets under its wings. (NNAM)

Center Right: Two bombs could be loaded under the wings just inboard of the main landing gear. One of the two air inlets for the jet engine is visible in the leading edge of the wing in this photograph. (NNAM)

Right: This General Electric J31 is on display at the National Naval Aviation Museum at NAS Pensacola, Florida. The small jet engine produced 1,600 pounds of static thrust which was enough for the Fireball to fly on without the help of the Wright R-1820-72W radial. However, the jet engine was primarily intended to operate in conjunction with the radial powerplant. (Kinzey)

RYAN XF2R-1 DARK SHARK

The XF2R Dark Shark was a further development of the FR-1 Fireball. It replaced the Wright radial engine with a General Electric XT-31-GE-2 turboprop powerplant mounted inside an extended nose. (NNAM)

Although the end of World War II caused the cancellation of all but sixty-six of the FR-1 Fireballs, the Navy authorized Ryan to convert one of these, BuNo. 39661, to a new configuration. The Wright R-1820-72W Cyclone radial engine was replaced with a General Electric XT-31-GE-2 turboprop which produced 1,700 horsepower and turned a large four-blade propeller. Designated the XF2R-1 by the Navy and named the Dark Shark, the reconfigured composite fighter first flew in November 1946 making it the first Navy aircraft to fly with a turboprop engine. The top speed rose to over 500 miles-per-hour, and although it was heavier than the FR-1, it was more maneuverable than the Fireball. The pitch

of the propeller could momentarily be set to reverse thrust in flight, thus causing the aircraft to rapidly decelerate. Engine response was much faster than with the radial engine, because turboprops essentially run at full rpm at all times. Power changes are made by moving the pitch of the propeller, so there is no need to wait for engine revolutions to increase.

In spite of the fact that the Dark Shark's performance was impressive for a composite fighter, the die had been cast in favor of new fighters powered only by turbojet engines. As a result, no production F2Rs were ever ordered.

A front view shows the elongated nose and the large four-blade propeller and spinner installed on the Dark Shark. (NNAM)

CURTISS XF15C-1 STINGAREE

The other composite fighter design to reach the flying prototype stage was the Curtiss XF15C-1 Stingaree. In its original con-figuration, it had a low-mounted horizontal tail. (NNAM)

Even as Curtiss was having problems with the XF14C that would eventually result in the cancellation of the program, the Navy issued the company a contract for another high-altitude fighter using both a radial engine and a small turbojet located in the center fuselage. It was hoped that a considerable increase in top speed performance could be gained with a composite engine design. On April 7, 1944, this contract was issued for three prototypes to be powered by a Pratt & Whitney R-2800-34W radial engine and an Allis-Chalmers J-36 jet engine, which was a license-built British design. Bureau numbers 01213, 01214, and 01215 were assigned. The large aircraft, designated the XF15C-1, featured a bubble canopy and a laminar flow wing to decrease drag and increase performance. Wingspan was 48 feet with more than 400 square feet of surface area. The length was 43 feet, 8 inches. The plane was to be built using a stronger new aluminum alloy, and it had an empty weight of 12,648 pounds. Maximum gross weight was 18,698 pounds.

The first of the three prototypes flew on February 28, 1945, with only the radial engine installed. The jet engine was installed during the first week of May, but the aircraft was destroyed in a crash on May 8. Flight testing was resumed on July 9 with the second prototype, but by then stability and vibration problems had been discovered. In an attempt to correct these problems, the entire tail assembly was redesigned, and the third prototype was the first to fly with the "T" tail design instead of having the horizontal tail mounted on the fuselage. This feature was then retrofitted to the second prototype. The vertical tail was also increased in area, but even after these changes were made, serious shortcomings persisted. By this time, composite power for fighter aircraft was losing favor with the Navy, and the decision to focus on all jet powered fighters also contributed to the demise of the Stingaree.

When the Navy cancelled the XF15C-1, it marked the last time Curtiss would build an aircraft for the Navy. The proud company, which bore the name of aviation pioneer Glenn Curtiss, had produced many outstanding designs for the U. S. military for many years. But in its final years, it had become plagued by numerous problems, and several of its World War II aircraft had gained a reputation for poor quality and workmanship. It was soon bankrupt and completely out of business.

The third prototype is seen here in its final con-figuration while assigned to the Naval Air Test Center at NAS Patuxent River, Maryland. The 215 on the fuselage is derived from the last three digits of the aircraft's Bureau number, 01215. Note that the spinner on the propeller has been deleted. By this time the red stripes had been added to the national insignia. (NNAM)

DIVE AND TORPEDO BOMBERS

Chapter 2

When the Japanese attacked Pearl Harbor, two Navy squadrons and one Marine squadron were still equipped with the Curtiss SBC Helldiver. This would be the last American biplane to be assigned to front line combat units. (NNAM)

It could be argued that the U. S. Navy dive bomber was the weapon that won the war in the Pacific, given the success of the SBD Dauntless at the Battle of Midway. Though the Navy entered the war with the belief that the best weapon against a large enemy combatant was the torpedo, the vulnerability of that type during its low and slow attack profile often prevented it from becoming the major factor in whether the battle was lost or won.

The Navy entered World War II with a few squadrons still operating biplane scout bombers in the form of the Curtiss SBC Helldiver. Although there were a number of other scout/dive bombers

Known as the "carrier killer," the Douglas SBD Dauntless scout bomber sank more Japanese shipping than any other American aircraft. Although replaced in most front line squadrons by the SB2C Helldiver during the final two years of the war, the Dauntless was in continual service throughout the war. (National Archives via Bell)

SB2C-1, Mod II, Helldivers prepare to launch from the second carrier to be named YORKTOWN, CV-10. The Helldiver's carrier trials aboard YORKTOWN were far from satisfactory, and it was plagued with problems throughout much of its operational life, earning it the rather unflattering nickname, "big tailed beast." But eventually the Helldiver's faults were corrected enough for it to give good service during the final two years of the war. (National Archives)

that saw operational service during the war, the most successful of the type was the Dauntless. Even though several follow on aircraft were designed after the Dauntless, developmental issues resulted in the SBD never being fully replaced, and it became one of a very few types that saw operational service from the first day of the war until the last.

This chapter takes a look at the dive and torpedo bombers that served with the U. S. Navy and Marine Corps during World War II. Included are all the dive and torpedo bomber types which were in operational combat squadrons when America entered the

war in December 1941, as are all aircraft of these two types which were developed and made their first flight during the war. All designs that made it to the flying prototype stage before the end of World War II are discussed, even if they did not achieve operational status.

The chapter concludes with a brief look at the final designs developed before the Navy changed its doctrine and strategy, leading to the development of attack aircraft after World War II came to an end.

Designed by Douglas as a replacement for their earlier SBD Dauntless, the two-seat XSB2D-1 was never put into production. Only two prototypes were built, one of which is shown here taking off on a test flight. The XSB2D-1 marked the end of the development of two-seat scout bombers. Subsequently, it was redesigned as a single-seat torpedo bomber designated the BTD-1, but only twenty-eight BTD-1s were produced. Douglas again modified the design to meet the evolving Navy requirements and doctrine, and this eventually resulted in the XBT2D-1. This aircraft was the prototype for what would become the famous Douglas AD Skyraider attack aircraft, and this new class of airplanes replaced both dive and torpedo bomber types. (NNAM)

CURTISS SBC HELLDIVER

SBC-3, BuNo. 0571, was the commander's aircraft for Scouting Squadron Three (VS-3). The white tail surfaces indicated assignment to USS SARATOGA, CV-3. Notice how the top deck of the rear fuselage collapsed to provide a better field of fire for the flexible machine gun. (NNAM)

Although originally designed as a monoplane fighter, the Curtiss SBC Helldiver was redesigned into a scout/dive bomber and gained the distinction of being the last combat biplane produced in the United States. Other American biplanes would continue to be used well into World War II, but they would serve in secondary supporting roles including observation, light transport, and training. The biplane had all but disappeared from U. S. combat units by the end of 1941, but VB-8 and VS-8, both assigned to the newly-commissioned aircraft carrier USS HORNET, CV-8, and Marine Squadron VMO-151 were still equipped with SBC Helldivers at the time of the Japanese attack on Pearl Harbor.

The original design of the aircraft was that of a two-seat fighter with a single parasol wing. Designated the XF12C-1, the aircraft first flew in this configuration in 1933. Shortly thereafter, the Navy decided it wanted a scouting aircraft instead, so the designation was changed to XS4C-1. The role was then changed to scout bomber, and the designation became XSBC-1. It remained a two-place design with the pilot in the front cockpit and radio operator/gunner in the rear cockpit. The aircraft was originally powered by a Wright R-1520-92 engine which produced 625 horsepower, but

This inflight photo of SBC-3, BuNo. 0543, provides a good look at the prewar markings on top of the yellow wing. This Helldiver was assigned to Scouting FIVE (VS-5) aboard USS YORKTOWN, CV-5. The tail surfaces were Insignia Red. This aircraft was in the fourth section, so the lower half of the cowling and the chevron on top of the wing were black. The aircraft number was on top of the wing as well as in the codes on the fuselage. (U. S Navy)

The air group commander for USS YORK-TOWN flew SBC-3, BuNo. 0527. In the pre-war years, which featured colorful paint schemes, aircraft assigned to YORKTOWN had red tail surfaces. The fuselage band was also red. Air group commanders often flew the scouting types of aircraft, because they had the longest range and endurance of any aircraft in the air group. This allowed the commander to remain on the scene the longest period of time to direct the air battle. Once the long-range fighters like the F6F Hellcat became available, commanders usually flew in a fighter. (NNAM)

this was changed to an R-1820-80 powerplant. During tests, the parasol wing failed due to high "G" stresses experienced during recoveries from dives, so the design was changed to a biplane.

Designated XSBC-2, the redesigned biplane first flew on December 9, 1934, and was powered by a Wright R-1520-12 engine which delivered 700 horsepower. The main landing gear retracted into wells in the forward fuselage, leaving the outer surfaces of the wheels and tires exposed. The tail gear also retracted into the aft fuselage. The top of the aft fuselage was a turtledeck which folded down to provide good fields of fire for the gunner with his flexible .30-caliber machine gun. The fuselage was of all metal construction, but the wings, flaps, ailerons, rudder, and elevators were all covered with fabric.

Another engine change to the Pratt & Whitney R-1535-82 was made in March 1936, and the prototype was redesignated XSBC-3. Now happy with the aircraft, the Navy ordered eighty-three production SBC-3s with R-1532-94 engines. This engine produced 825 horsepower for takeoff and 750 horsepower at 9,500 feet. The order was placed in August 1936, and deliveries began less than a year later in July 1937. It was given the nickname Helldiver, a name which had previously been used by an earlier Curtiss aircraft designated the F8C. Armament consisted of a single fixed .30-caliber machine gun in the cowling and one flexible .30-caliber machine gun in the rear cockpit. A 500-pound bomb could be carried beneath the fuselage, and a displacement yoke insured that it would safely clear the arc of the propeller when it was released. Alternatively, a 45-gallon external fuel tank to extend scouting

range could be carried on the centerline station. Smaller bombs could be loaded on racks under each lower wing section.

The first production SBC-3s were assigned to VS-5 aboard USS YORKTOWN. Later, VS-3 in SARATOGA and VS-6 aboard ENTERPRISE received SBC-3s. Additionally, Fighting SIX (VF-6) aboard ENTERPRISE operated one SBC-3, and Bombing THREE (VB-3) and Fighting THREE, (VF-3) aboard SARATOGA each had a single SBC-3 assigned.

Development of a more powerful version of the Helldiver began when the 76th production SBC-3 was fitted with a 950-horsepower Wright R-1820-22 engine that turned a three-blade Hamilton Standard propeller. This prototype was designated the XSBC-4.

The final production version was the SBC-4, and it had a Wright R-1820-34 engine which delivered 950 horsepower for takeoff and 750 horsepower at 15,000 feet. This enabled the Helldiver to carry a 1,000-pound bomb on the centerline station. The first of 124 SBC-4s was delivered to the fleet in March 1939, and the last entered Navy service in April 1941. An additional fifty were provided to France. Interestingly, the French aircraft had self-sealing fuel tanks, while those for the U. S. Navy did not. SBC-4s had a top speed of 237 miles-per-hour and a cruising speed of 127 miles-per-hour. The ceiling was 27,300 feet, and the final version of the Helldiver had a range of 590 miles while carrying a 500-pound bomb.

France surrendered to Germany before their SBC-4s could be delivered in country, and they never became operational. An interesting footnote concerning the fifty French aircraft is that five

The Marines also flew Helldivers. This SBC-4 was assigned to the First Marine Air Wing in 1940. An external fuel tank is carried in place of a bomb on the centerline station. (NNAM)

This photo of SBC-4, BuNo. 1318, on final approach provides a good look at the underside details of the Helldiver. This aircraft was assigned to a Navy Reserve unit, and the tail, fuselage band, and cowling were painted green. The 45-gallon external fuel tank was often carried on Helldivers. (U. S. Navy)

wound up with the Royal Air Force where they were called Cleveland Mk. Is. These aircraft were never used operationally, but they did serve as ground trainers for maintenance personnel with the RAF.

The first U. S. Navy squadron to receive the SBC-4 was VS-2 aboard USS LEXINGTON, CV-2. But VS-2 replaced these aircraft with SBD-2 Dauntlesses in 1941. VB-8 and VS-8 aboard the new USS HORNET, CV-8, were the only carrier-based squadrons to be equipped with SBC-4s at the time of the Japanese attack on Pearl Harbor, but these were also quickly replaced with Dauntlesses before HORNET saw any combat.

The Marine Corps had a total of twenty-three SBC-4s in its inventory on December 7, 1941. Twelve of these were assigned to

Marine Observation Squadron 151 (VMO-151) at MCAS Quantico, Virginia. In May 1942, this squadron was sent to Tutuila Island in American Samoa. In September 1942, the squadron was redesignated VMSB-151, and the following month it was divided into two squadrons, VMSB-151 and VMO-155. VMSB-151's SBC-4s would be replaced with Dauntlesses by June of 1943, and this would mark the end of the SBC-4 in any scouting/bombing squadron. They would remain in training and other support roles until 1944.

The SBC was not the first Curtiss aircraft to be named Helldiver, nor would it be the last. The name was passed on to the SB2C, and that aircraft would see plenty of combat before the Japanese finally surrendered in September 1945.

One of the two Navy bombing squadrons still equipped with SBC-4s at the time of the Japanese attack on Pearl Harbor was VB-8. This SBC-4 is painted in the overall Light Gray paint scheme and was assigned to VB-8 in 1941. (NNAM)

Before America entered the war, most Helldivers had been replaced in front line squadrons with SBD Dauntlesses, but many remained in service in training units. This SBC-4 is painted in the Blue-Gray over Light Gray scheme and has markings used in early 1942. (NNAM)

DOUGLAS TBD-1 DEVASTATOR

The XTBD-1 prototype had a lower canopy design than the later production aircraft. The vertical tail also had a different shape and size. A bomb is carried on the centerline station, denoting the aircraft's secondary role as a horizontal bomber. (NNAM)

The first carrier-based monoplane ordered by the U. S. Navy was the Douglas TBD-1 Devastator torpedo bomber. Developed in 1934, the prototype XTBD-1 made its first flight on April 15, 1935. Except for the control surfaces, the aircraft was covered by a metal skin, and the outer panels of the wing were corrugated metal. These outer panels could be folded hydraulically to save room for carrier storage. The three crew members, including the pilot, assistant pilot/bombardier, and radio operator/gunner, were housed in tandem beneath a long greenhouse canopy. The canopy had a very low profile on the prototype, but the height was increased on the production aircraft. The prototype was powered by a Pratt & Whitney XR-1830-60 engine which developed 800 horsepower for take off.

The Navy placed an order for 114 production TBD-1s on February 3, 1936, and these differed from the prototype by having the higher windscreen and canopy, a redesigned vertical tail, and the installation of a R-1830-64 engine which was rated at 900 horsepower. Although called a torpedo bomber and capable of carrying a single 2,000-pound torpedo in a semi-recessed bay beneath the fuselage, the TBD-1 could also serve as a horizontal bomber. A 1,000-pound bomb or three 500-pound bombs could be carried under the fuselage, or up to twelve 100-pound bombs could be loaded under the wings outboard of the semi-retractable landing gear. A fixed .30-caliber machine gun was mounted in the cowling on the right side of the aircraft, while a single .30-caliber flexible machine gun was manned by the radio operator/gunner in the rear

TBD-1, BuNo. 0391, served as aircraft number 7 in VT-5 aboard USS YORKTOWN, CV-5, during the prewar years. It displays YORKTOWN's Insignia Red tail, and as the section leader of the squadron's third section, the cowl ring and fuselage band are Insignia Blue. The large E on the fuselage indicates the squadron won the Excellence Award for the previous year. (U. S. Navy)

Three Devastators from Torpedo Squadron Two (VT-2) fly in formation over the California coast. VT-2 was assigned to USS LEXINGTON, CV-2. This photograph clearly shows the higher canopy on the production aircraft. The fact that these aircraft do not have the teardrop-shaped fairing on their forward fuselage indicates that they retain the original fixed .30-caliber machine gun. (NNAM)

As was the case with a few F2A-1 Buffalos assigned to VF-3, the Navy applied several different experimental camouflage schemes to TBD-1 Devastators assigned to VT-3. A temporary water-based paint was used. These were known as Mc-Clelland Barclay camouflage schemes, and Design 7 is seen here on TBD-1, BuNo. 0320. This photograph was taken at NAS North Island on August 22, 1940. (NNAM)

In 1939, TBD-1, BuNo. 0268, was fitted with floats, as the Navy experimented with floatplane versions of several carrier-based aircraft. This Devastator was redesignated TBD-1A, but no production version of the floatplane version was ordered. (U. S. Navy)

cockpit. On some aircraft, the fixed cowl gun was later changed to a .50-caliber weapon. At the Battle of Midway, Devastators in VT-6 and VT-8 had their single flexible guns replaced with dual mounts.

The R-1830-64 left the Devastator considerably underpowered. Top speed was only 206 miles-per-hour, and cruising speed was 128 miles-per-hour. When loaded with a torpedo, the aircraft's manual recommended a reduced fuel load, but it could fly with a full fuel load in an overweight configuration. To save weight when carrying a torpedo, the usual practice was to leave the bombardier behind and fly with only the pilot and radio operator/gunner.

Deliveries to the fleet began on October 5, 1937, with VT-3 aboard SARATOGA being the first unit to receive the new monoplane. VT-2 in LEXINGTON, VT-5 in YORKTOWN, and VT-6 in ENTERPRISE soon followed. Later, VT-8 received TBD-1s aboard HORNET, and squadrons with a reduced number of Devastators were assigned to the smaller carriers, RANGER and WASP. A second contract for fifteen additional TBD-1s increased the number of production aircraft to 129, but thirty of these were destroyed in operational accidents before the U. S. entered World War II. The first production aircraft, BuNo. 0268, was temporarily fitted with floats for evaluation as a floatplane, and in this configuration, it was designated TBD-1A

The Devastator got its first taste of combat on January 10, 1942, when two TBD-1s from VT-2 aboard USS LEXINGTON, CV-2, launched to attack a Japanese I-class submarine near Johnson Island, approximately 800-miles southwest of Pearl Harbor. Each

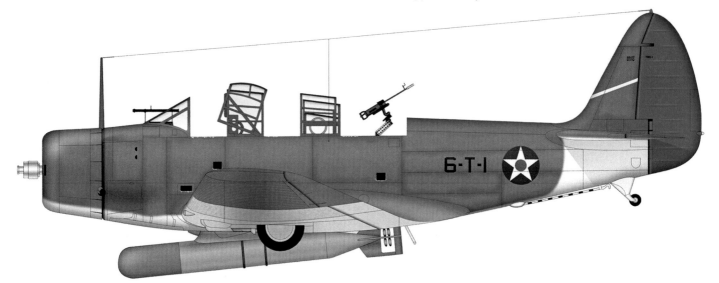

TBD-1 Devastator, BuNo. 0370, was flown by Lieutenant Commander Eugene E. Lindsey, commanding officer of Torpedo Squadron SIX, when he led his squadron from USS ENTERPRISE to attack Japanese carriers reported to be south of Oahu on December 7th, 1941. To reduce aircraft visibility, the overall Light Gray paint scheme had been superseded by the Blue-Gray over Light Gray scheme, the national insignias were smaller and appeared in only four locations, and squadron insignias were not usually displayed on the aircraft. Note how the Non-specular Blue-Gray was also applied to the bottom of the outer wings, making the aircraft less visible from the air when it was on the deck with its wings folded. This TBD-1 was lost in an operational accident while attempting to land aboard ENTERPRISE on May 28, 1942, but Lt. Cdr. Lindsey and his crew were rescued by the destroyer MONAGHAN, DD-354, and returned to ENTERPRISE. A few days later, Lt. Cdr. Lindsey was killed while leading his squadron against the Japanese carrier force during the Battle of Midway. (Artwork by Rock Roszak)

aircraft carried two 325-pound depth charges. The submarine was only slightly damaged.

On January 11, SARATOGA was hit by a torpedo and had to return to Pearl Harbor. The carrier's air group, including VT-3, was flown ashore and remained in Hawaii while the ship returned to the west coast for repairs.

The U. S. Navy began offensive operations with its carriers on February 1, 1942, with a series of hit-and-run raids. ENTERPRISE attacked enemy ships and installations at Kwajalein and Wotje. Nine of VT-6's TBDs were loaded with bombs, while the other nine carried torpedoes. Flying with SBDs from VB-6 and VS-6, and covered by F4F-3 Wildcat fighters from VF-6, the air group attacked the Japanese with moderate success. All of the Devastators returned safely to ENTERPRISE, but five SBDs were lost.

On the same day, YORKTOWN's air group struck Jaluit with marginal results. The weather was poor, and six aircraft were lost, four of these being TBD-1s. Loaded with standard bombs, the TBD-1s and Dauntlesses caused relatively light damage to two Japanese ships.

On February 24, ENTERPRISE attacked the Japanese at Wake Island. VT-6's role in this raid was to drop 100-pound bombs on oil tanks, and each Devastator carried twelve bombs. The TBD-1s dropped their bomb loads from 12,000 feet, but they achieved only limited success.

ENTERPRISE attacked Marcus Island on March 4, but no Devastators participated in the raid. The "Big E" then returned to Pearl Harbor prior to joining up with HORNET for the Doolittle/Halsey Raid on Tokyo. During that operation, VT-6's Devastators flew patrols along with Dauntlesses of VB-6 and VS-6.

Meanwhile, both LEXINGTON and YORKTOWN moved south to New Guinea and launched strikes against Lae and Salamaua. VT-2 carried out a torpedo attack against Japanese shipping on March 10, and sank a transport, but most of the torpedoes malfunctioned as was common early in the war. On the same day, VT-5 participated with YORKTOWN's air group as horizontal bombers. Releasing their bombs from 13,000 feet, the Devastators damaged a seaplane tender. SBDs from the two carriers also scored hits, and a total of three ships were sunk.

By early May, the two carriers were operating in the Solomon Islands. On May 4, they attacked the Japanese at Tulagi with VT-5 launching two torpedo attacks. Again, the brave crews were betrayed by faulty torpedoes, but they were able to score one good

In April 1942, USS WASP, CV-7, arrived at Scapa Flow in the Orkney Islands. While the carrier transported British aircraft to the island of Malta, the TBD-1s assigned to that small carrier's reduced torpedo squadron were put ashore to fly anti-submarine patrols against German U-boats. Two of VT-7's Devastators are shown here at Scapa Flow. They are painted in the Blue-Gray over Light Gray scheme and carry larger national insignia at six locations and thirteen red and white stripes on the rudder. These markings were instituted in January 1942 to make the aircraft more identifiable as American in the heat of battle. (NNAM)

hit and damage an enemy destroyer. The raid also damaged several transports.

The first major engagement between the U. S. and Japanese fleets took place in the Coral Sea between May 4 and 8, 1942. This would also become the first naval battle in history where the opposing ships never came in sight of each other. Instead, it would be fought entirely by aircraft. The air groups from LEXINGTON and YORKTOWN attacked the Japanese, and on May 7, VT-2 and VT-5 shared the credit with Dauntless scout bombers for the sinking of the light carrier SHOHO. On May 8, the two torpedo squadrons joined with the Dauntlesses again to damage the larger fleet carrier SHOKAKU, one of the Japanese carriers that had attacked Pearl Harbor.

The U. S. Navy suffered the loss of LEXINGTON during the

During the first half of 1942, Devastators were used as horizontal bombers for some of the carrier raids against Japanese installations on islands across the Pacific. This underside view of a TBD-1, taken as it approached its carrier for a landing, shows the attachment points for bombs under the fuselage and wings. Bombs up to the 500-pound size could be carried on each of the two hardpoints beneath the fuselage, while a smaller 100-pound bomb could be loaded on each of the twelve attachment points under the wings. A single 1000-pound bomb could also be carried under the fuselage. (National Archives)

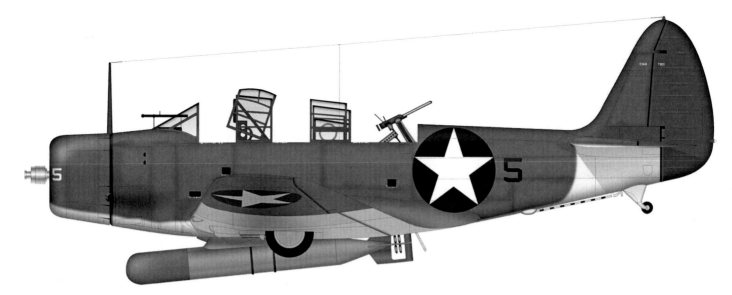

TBD-1 Devastator, BuNo. 0368, was assigned to VT-6 aboard USS ENTERPRISE, CV-6, at the Battle of Midway, June 4, 1942. The crew was composed of the pilot ENS Irvin H. McPherson and Radio Operator/Gunner ARM2c Don Horton. Note the change to the dual defensive gun configuration made prior to the battle. Compare the markings on this aircraft to the prior photograph. To prevent confusion with Japanese aircraft in combat, the red and white rudder markings were removed and the national insignia no longer included the red disc in the center of the white star. (Artwork by Rock Roszak)

Battle of the Coral Sea, and as the carrier sank, she took eleven of her Devastators to the bottom with her.

Although heavily damaged, YORKTOWN steamed back to Pearl Harbor for repairs. After a very brief yard period lasting only seventy-two hours, she raced to join HORNET and ENTERPRISE near Midway Island where the Japanese were expected to attack next. SARATOGA's VT-3 replaced VT-5 in YORKTOWN as the carrier departed for Midway.

On June 4, the three American carriers launched aircraft to attack Admiral Nagumo's carrier force with its four fleet carriers, AKAGI, KAGA, SORYU, and HIRYU. Included were fifteen Devastators of HORNET's VT-8, fourteen from VT-6 aboard ENTERPRISE, and twelve from VT-3 in YORKTOWN. Only six F4F-4 Wildcats from VF-3 were available to escort the slow torpedo bombers.

The attack was intended to be coordinated with Dauntless scout bombers diving on the enemy from above at the same time the torpedo bombers carried out their torpedo drops from low level. This would divide the Japanese anti-aircraft fire, and fighters would defend the attacking bombers from enemy A6M2 Zeros. But it did not work out that way. The squadrons became separated, so, running low on fuel, each attacked alone.

First to go in was VT-8 which attacked SORYU. One by one, Japanese fighters splashed the slow Devastators. The addition of a second .30-caliber machine gun in the rear cockpit did little to help. Every one of the squadron's TBD-1s were shot down, and all crew members perished except for one pilot, Ensign George Gay.

VT-6 was next to attack, and Lt. Cdr. Eugene E. Lindsey led his squadron against the carrier KAGA. Also alone and without fighter cover, VT-6 fared little better than VT-8. Scoring no hits, only three Devastators survived to return to ENTERPRISE, while a fourth ditched near the carrier, and its crew was rescued. Like VT-8, the TBD-1s of VT-6 had dual .30-caliber machine guns in their rear cockpits, but without fighter cover, these guns alone were simply not enough to protect the slow Devastators.

HIRYU was attacked by VT-3, and although there were a few F4F-4 Wildcats to help protect these torpedo bombers, they simply were not enough. Further, VT-3's Devastators still had only one flexible gun in the rear cockpit for self defense. Only one of the twelve TBD-1s from VT-3 made it safely back to YORKTOWN.

The brave crews of these squadrons were betrayed again by faulty torpedoes. Giving their lives in the process, they delivered weapons that failed to run true and detonate against their targets. But their sacrifice was not in vain, and their contribution to the overall success of the battle was significant. As they attacked at low level, the Devastators pulled the fighter cover above the Japanese fleet down to low level. Minutes after the last Devastator made its run at its target, Dauntlesses arrived over the Japanese carrier force almost unopposed. They screamed down on the Japanese carriers, and within five minutes, AKAGI, KAGA, and SORYU were burning hulks. The following day, Dauntlesses finished off HIRYU, and four of the six carriers that had attacked Pearl Harbor only six months earlier were at the bottom of the Pacific.

On June 6, the three surviving TBD-1s from VT-6 launched from ENTERPRISE to search for the cruisers MIKUMA and MOGAMI. Based on previously determined rules of engagement intended to preserve the few remaining torpedo bombers, these Devastators did not attack the enemy cruisers. However, SBD's sank MIKUMA, and MOGAMI limped away severely damaged. When the three Devastators returned from this mission, it marked the end of the TBD-1's combat career. The remaining Devastators were relegated to training and hack duties until they too were stricken from the Navy's inventory.

Because the Devastators were slaughtered by the Japanese at Midway, the aircraft has come under much criticism. Certainly, it was obsolete by the time the war started, and it lacked self-sealing fuel tanks and other features considered essential for combat aircraft. But they served well in combat up until that time, and it should also be remembered that five of the six TBF-1 Avengers which participated in the Battle of Midway were shot down. The sixth was severely damaged, but it limped back to Midway Island where it was written off as being beyond repair. Yet the Avenger went on to be one of the most successful aircraft of World War II.

A Mark II, Model 2 telescopic gun sight was mounted through the windscreen just to the right of centerline. The pilot used this sight when firing the fixed machine gun located in the right side of the cowling. This gun was used to fire at the target being attacked by the TBD-1 in an effort to suppress anti-aircraft fire. The primitive gun sight was not very effective, and it had a tendency to fog up during temperature changes. (NNAM)

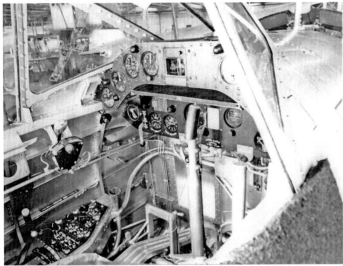

The instrument panel in the Devastator was a two-level design. It was painted an anti-glare flat black and contained basic flying and engine instruments. The control column was a simple design with a black control grip at the top. (NNAM)

A low view inside the pilot's cockpit provides a better look at the two different levels of the instrument panel. There was no floor in the cockpit. Instead, the pilot's feet were placed on guides that ran between the seat and each of the two rudder pedals. (NNAM)

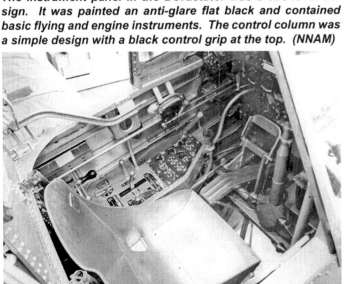

The throttle quadrant with its engine controls was mounted high on the left side of the pilot's cockpit. The electrical control panel was at the forward end of the console, and the trim tab controls and the fuel selector valve were further aft on the console. In the pre-war era, cockpits in the TBD-1 were silver, but they were painted Interior Green when the colorful pre-war paint schemes were replaced with low visibility camouflage paint on the exterior surfaces of the aircraft. (NNAM)

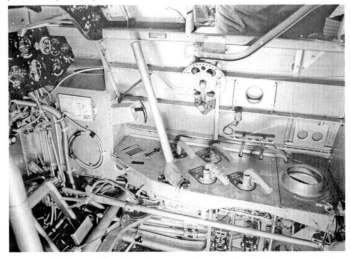

The large lever on the right side of the pilot's cockpit was the hydraulic hand pump. The crank with the large round plate opened and closed the cockpit enclosure. There were four large valves on the console. Of the two nearest the edge of the console, the forward one controlled the landing gear and the one aft of it was for the wing flaps. The forward valve of two nearer the fuselage wall was for the parking brake and the one aft of it operated the hydraulic wing fold mechanism. (NNAM)

SECOND PILOT'S COCKPIT

The middle cockpit was officially called the second pilot's cockpit, and it had basic flight controls and instruments. On bombing missions it was occupied by the bombardier, but no bombardier was required for a torpedo attack. Because the torpedo was so heavy, the middle cockpit was usually left unoccupied to help save weight whenever one of these weapons was carried. These are the instruments in the middle cockpit in an early TBD-1. They include a ball for turn coordination at the top, a magnetic compass, an altimeter, and an air speed indicator. Later, a standard rate of turn needle was added above the ball. (NNAM)

Very little was located on the sides of the middle cockpit. Nothing that was essential to the aircraft's operation was installed in this cockpit, because it was often unoccupied. There was no floor, allowing the bombardier to crouch down in the bottom of the fuselage to use the bomb sight. (NNAM)

A cylinder which inflated the wing flotation bags with CO_2 was mounted on the right side of the middle cockpit. These bags were intended to keep the aircraft afloat in the event of a ditching, but they were removed once the war began to prevent a ditched aircraft from falling into the hands of the enemy. (NNAM)

A Norden bomb sight was located in the lower fuselage below the pilot's seat. This top secret device was used when the Devastator was employed as a horizontal bomber. To use the sight, the bombardier had to crawl down into the lower fuselage, then stretch forward on his stomach to assume a very cramped and uncomfortable position. He aimed the bomb sight through an angled glass window. Before this could happen, two doors in the bottom of the fuselage, located just forward of the window, had to be opened using the small crank seen just above the top right corner of the window. (NNAM)

RADIO OPERATOR/GUNNER'S COCKPIT

The radio operator/gunner sat in a seat which was attached to a swiveling ring. It could be rotated a full 360-degrees around the ring. The four items in the holes in the floor were lighted flotation marker buoys. (NNAM)

The left side of the radio operator/gunner's cockpit is shown here. The reel for the trailing wire antenna is visible on the side of the cockpit. (NNAM)

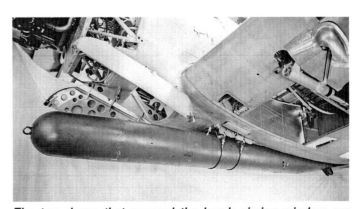

The flexible Browning .30-caliber machine gun was mounted on a separate perforated ring which was attached to the sides of the seat ring. The mount could be rolled across the ring, allowing the gun to be moved over an arc of almost 180-degrees. Further, the gun could be moved both vertically and horizontally on its "Y" shaped mounting bracket. Ammunition boxes were placed in the holder to the left of the gun. The gun stowed in the slot on the top of the fuselage, and this was covered by two hinged doors. At Midway, TBD-1s of VT-6 and VT-8 had their single flexible guns replaced by dual .30-caliber machine gun mounts. (NNAM)

TORPEDO DETAILS

A single aerial torpedo could be carried externally in a recessed area under the fuselage. American torpedoes, used in the early stages of World War II, were plagued with problems, and they often failed to explode after airmen gave their lives to deliver them against enemy ships. (NNAM)

The two doors that covered the bomb aiming window are shown here in the open position. Although a torpedo is shown in place in this view, the doors were opened to allow use of the bomb sight only when the Devastator was being used as a horizontal bomber to deliver conventional bomb loads. (NNAM)

VOUGHT SB2U VINDICATOR

The XSB2U-1 prototype, BuNo. 9725, made its first flight on January 4, 1936, and it is shown here a few months later on May 5. Production Vindicators differed little from the prototype, but most noticeably, the XSB2U-1 lacked the large scoop on the upper right side of the cowling. (NNAM)

In the mid-1930s the advantages the monoplane offered over the biplane had been established, but there were still many unknowns. Issues involving the wing loading and stability of monoplane designs remained as concerns, and the Navy used a double redundancy aircraft development program to ensure that reliable aircraft would continue to enter its inventory. First, new prototypes of both monoplane and biplane designs were ordered. Should severe problems be encountered with the monoplanes, the biplanes could be developed instead. Second, competing monoplane designs were requested from several contractors to increase the chances that at least one would prove successful. In the event that more than one of the designs were acceptable, the Navy also had the additional benefit of being able to choose the best. It was also thought that by having several aircraft design teams develop proposals, the new monoplane technologies could be advanced more rapidly.

As was discussed previously in the section on the TBD-1 Devastator, Douglas developed the Navy's first monoplane torpedo bomber which also became the first monoplane of any type to be acquired by the U. S. Navy for use aboard carriers. But the Navy also wanted monoplane scout bombers, and orders were placed for prototypes from Northrop, Brewster, and Vought. Vought's design was designated XSB2U-1, and as a contingency, Vought also received a contract for the prototype of a new biplane scout bomber designated the XSB3U-1.

The XSB2U-1 was a low-wing monoplane with retractable main gear that rotated ninety degrees as it folded back into wells under the wing. Vought would also use this same basic design on the F4U Corsair. To reduce size on aircraft carriers, the outer wing panels could be folded upward along a hinge line outboard of the landing gear and flaps. The prototype first flew on January 4, 1936, and early flight testing of both the XSB2U-1 and XSB3U-1 clearly established the superiority of the monoplane design. As a result, the biplane was cancelled, and an order for fifty-four production SB2U-1s was placed on October 26, 1936. Deliveries began in December 1937, with VB-3 aboard USS SARATOGA, CV-3, being the first squadron to receive the Navy's new monoplane scout bomber.

The SB2U-1 differed from the prototype by having a relocated forward antenna mast and repositioned exhaust ports. The canopy framing was strengthened, and the production aircraft had a large air scoop for both the oil cooler and carburetor located on the upper right side of the cowling.

The SB2U-1 was powered by a Pratt & Whitney R-1535-96 Twin-Wasp Junior radial engine which produced 825 horsepower and turned a two-blade, constant-speed propeller. The pitch of

The first squadron to become operational with the Navy's first monoplane scout bomber was VB-3. Known as the both the "Top Hats" and the "High Hats," the squadron was assigned to USS SARATOGA, CV-3. Painted in the colorful pre-war paint scheme, these new SB2U-1s are being prepared for a training mission on the carrier's flight deck in February 1938, only three months after the first production aircraft were delivered to the Navy. The SB2U-1 was powered by a Pratt & Whitney R-1535-96 engine which developed 825 horsepower. A total of fifty-four SB2U-1s were completed, and these were followed by fifty-eight SB2U-2s which were almost identical to the first version. (NNAM)

the propeller could also be changed to a negative angle so that it could be used as an air brake during a dive. Armament consisted of one fixed .30-caliber machine gun mounted inside the leading edge of the right wing and a flexible .30-caliber machine gun in the rear cockpit. A bomb up to the 1,000-pound size or depth charges could be carried on the centerline station, and a displacement yoke insured that the weapon would clear the arc of the propeller when dropped in a dive. For scouting missions, an external fuel tank could be carried in place of the bomb to increase range. Smaller bombs, usually in the 100-pound class, could be carried on underwing racks just outboard of the landing gear.

Some references have stated that the aircraft was an all-metal design, but this is not true. While the forward fuselage was covered with sheet metal, almost the entire aft fuselage was covered by fabric as was much of the wing panels. All control surfaces were likewise covered with fabric.

An order for fifty-eight SB2U-2s was placed in January 1938, and these were entering squadron service by the end of that year. Only minor equipment changes differentiated the SB2U-2 from the SB2U-1. VB-4 aboard RANGER took delivery of early production SB2U-2s in December 1938. By the end of 1940, VB-2, VB-3, VB-4, VS-41, VS-42, VS-71 and VS-72 were all equipped with SB2U-1s or SB2U-2s. Quite often, both versions were used simultaneously in the same squadron.

When the Japanese attacked Pearl Harbor and other military installations on Oahu on December 7, 1941, seven USMC Vindicators assigned to VMSB-231 were destroyed by strafing A6M2 Zeros at Ewa Field southwest of Pearl Harbor. By that time, the Navy dive and scouting squadrons aboard LEXINGTON, CV-2, and SARATOGA, CV-3 had replaced their Vindicators with SBD Dauntlesses. In the Atlantic, RANGER operated with her two squadrons of Vindicators, VS-41 and VS-42, during the months immediately following America's entry into the war. Aboard WASP, VS-71 and VS-72, also flew routine patrol missions while that carrier operated in the Atlantic. WASP was transferred to the Pacific after transporting British aircraft to Malta, and her Vindicators were replaced with Dauntlesses. By the time RANGER participated in Operation Torch in November 1942, her SB2Us had also been re-

SB2U-1, BuNo. 0757, was assigned to the squadron commander of Bombing TWO aboard USS LEXINGTON, CV-2. The tail color was Lemon Yellow, and the cowl ring and fuselage band were Insignia Red. The fuselage was painted silver, and the top of the wings were yellow with red chevron stripes. (U. S. Navy)

placed with SBDs. VS-9 trained with Vindicators aboard the escort carrier, USS CHARGER, AVG-30, in 1942 as they prepared for duty with Air Group 9, destined to be assigned to USS ESSEX, CV-9. However, the squadron transitioned to SBD-4 Dauntlesses before embarking in ESSEX. By September 1942, all Vindicators had been replaced with Dauntlesses in Navy squadrons.

One SB2U-1, BuNo. 0779, was converted to a floatplane and designated the XSB2U-3. After its conversion to a floatplane, the floats caused some directional stability problems, so a fin was added under the aft fuselage. This aircraft carried Navy markings. Most references state that this was the only Vindicator to be fitted with floats, but this is not the case. The first production SB2U-3, BuNo. 2044, was also fitted with floats and evaluated as a floatplane. It carried Marine markings, but all SB2U-3s that followed were equipped with conventional landing gear.

The SB2U-3 was the first version to be officially called Vindicator, but the name was then applied to all aircraft in the series. The SB2U-3 was developed specifically for the Marine Corps, and it had an R-1535-02 engine which produced 825 horsepower. It also had a greater internal fuel capacity than the earlier versions

SB2U-1, BuNo. 0779, was converted to the XSB2U-3 float plane. During the late 1930s, the Navy tested several of its aircraft designs with floats as a contingency in the event it was faced with a shortage of aircraft carriers after the war began. Had enough carriers not been available, the Navy considered operating aircraft from harbors and lagoons throughout the Pacific. In addition to the XSB2U-3, a Wildcat fighter, a Devastator torpedo bomber, and the XSB2C-2 Helldiver bomber were all evaluated as float planes. However, America's industrial might provided the Navy with enough aircraft carriers, and none of these types were ever put into production as float planes. (NNAM)

The first production SB2U-3, BuNo. 2044, was also fitted with floats. It had Marine markings and displays the fin beneath the aft fuselage in this photo. Also note the small rudders on the aft end of these floats and the differences in the struts which mount them to the aircraft as compared to the ones in the previous photograph. However, as was the case with the floatplane experiments with the Wildcat, Vindicator, and Helldiver, no floatplane version of the Vindicator was ever put into production. (NNAM)

The SB2U-2 differed little from the previous SB2U-1. BuNo. 1357 was assigned to the squadron commander of VS-72 aboard USS WASP, CV-7. The tail on this Vindicator was painted black, the color used during the pre-war years for aircraft assigned to WASP. (U. S. Navy)

The SB2U-3 was a dedicated Marine version of the Vindicator, and fifty-seven were built. They were assigned to Marine squadrons VMS-1 and VMS-2, but these two units were subsequently redesignated VMSB-231 and VMSB-241 respectively. This SB2U-3 was assigned to VMS-2, and it was painted in the overall Light Gray scheme used between December 1940 and October 1941. (U. S. Navy)

to increase range. The .30-caliber machine guns of the SB2U-1 and SB2U-2 were replaced with .50-caliber weapons. Up to four .50-caliber machine guns could be installed in the wings, but typically, only one was carried. Armor protection was provided for the crew. The span and area of the horizontal tail was increased by almost two feet. All of these changes resulted in an empty weight that was 921 pounds heavier than that of the SB2U-2, and this degraded the performance of the aircraft.

The most notable use of the Vindicator in combat was at Mid-

Underside details of the Vindicator are revealed in this photograph. The main landing gear retracted back into wells, rotating ninety degrees as it did. The tail hook was mounted externally just forward of the tail wheel. The pitot probe was near the left wing tip. A gun camera was mounted in the leading edge of the left wing, while a single .30-caliber machine gun was in the right wing. This Vindicator is carrying an external fuel tank on its centerline station. (U. S. Navy)

way when twenty-one SB2U-3s were reassigned from VMSB-231 to VMSB-241 to become part of the defending force on the island. On June 4, 1942, twelve of these aircraft took off from Midway to attack the Japanese fleet as part of a major strike consisting of Army and Marine aircraft. One Vindicator turned back because of mechanical problems, but the other eleven attacked the Japanese ships with 500-pound bombs. They scored no hits on the enemy and two of the SB2U-3s were lost. A third ran out of fuel and ditched on the way back to Midway, but the crew was rescued.

The following day, six SBD-2 Dauntlesses and six SB2U-3s took off for a follow-up attack, but the target could not be found in the poor weather. While returning to Midway, one of the Vindicators suddenly plunged into the sea, and the crew was lost. On June 5, the remaining Dauntlesses and Vindicators of VMSB-241 participated in the attack on the cruisers MOGAMI and MIKUMA. Captain Richard E. Flemming led VMSB-241's second section in the attack. His SB2U-3 was hit by anti-aircraft fire, but Flemming pressed home his attack. He scored a near miss with his bomb, then his burning Vindicator crashed into the sea. For his part in this action, Captain Flemming was posthumously awarded the Medal of Honor.

Three Vindicators remained on Midway after the battle, but none were ever used again in combat. Today, only one Vindicator remains, and it has been restored and is on display at the National Naval Aviation Museum aboard NAS Pensacola, Florida.

Although of poor quality, this rare color photograph is a single frame taken from a movie reel and shows two SB2U-3 Vindicators of VMSB-241 taking off from Midway Island to search for and attack the Japanese. VMSB-241 had a mix of nineteen SBD-2 Dauntless and twenty-one SB2U-3 Vindicator scout-bombers at Midway and lost fourteen of these aircraft during the battle. (NNAM)

VINDICATOR DETAILS

The National Naval Aviation Museum at Pensacola, Florida, has restored an SB2U-2 Vindicator to original condition. Details of the pilot's instrument panel are revealed in this view. (Kinzey)

Some of the radio gear in the rear cockpit is shown here. Note the key for sending Morse code on the deck to the right. The green bottle contained breathing oxygen for the radio operator/gunner. (Kinzey)

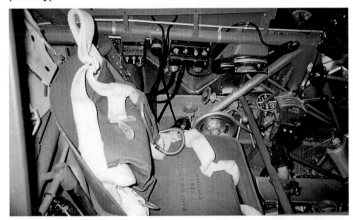

Details on the left side of the pilot's cockpit included the throttle quadrant, trim wheels, and the fuel tank selector valve. The red tubing is a control lock which prevented the control surfaces from being moved when the aircraft was parked. (Kinzey)

Various switches and knobs were on the electrical distribution panel on the right side of the pilot's cockpit. The pilot's oxygen bottle is also visible in this view as is the handle for the hydraulic hand pump. Flap controls were on the black triangular shaped panel. (Kinzey)

The centerline bomb rack with its anti-sway braces and the bomb yoke displacement gear are illustrated in this close-up. Note also the windows in the bottom of the fuselage just forward of the leading edge of the wing. Many Navy aircraft of this era had similar windows so the pilot could see what was below his aircraft. (Kinzey)

In addition to the large bomb on the centerline rack, smaller bombs of the 100-pound class could be loaded on a rack under each wing. For scouting missions these were often the only bombs carried. This photograph also provides a good look at the left main landing gear. (Kinzey)

BREWSTER XSBA-1 & SBN-1

In its original form, the XSBA-1 prototype, BuNo. 9726, featured a low canopy which covered its two cockpits. It was powered by a Wright R-1820-4 engine which turned a two-blade propeller, and it was the first aircraft produced by the Brewster Aeronautical Corporation. (NNAM)

As mentioned in the previous section on the SB2U Vindicator, the Navy asked several aircraft manufacturers to develop monoplane designs for scout bombers. One of the competing designs was ordered from Brewster on October 14, 1934, and the prototype was designated XSBA-1. As was standard for Navy designations, the X stood for experimental, the SB for scout bomber, and the A was the manufacturer's designation for the new Brewster Aeronautical Corporation. In fact, the XSBA-1 would become the company's first aircraft. It had many similar design features with the F2A Buffalo fighter which Brewster developed concurrently with the XSBA-1.

Unlike the other early scout bomber monoplane designs which had wings mounted low on the fuselage, Brewster chose a mid-mounted configuration. The landing gear was located under the wings, but it retracted into wells in the sides of the fuselage. A Wright R-1820-4 engine was originally installed under a large cowling, and it turned a two-blade propeller. This engine was soon replaced with a XR-1820-22 that provided 950 horsepower. The more powerful engine was installed under a shorter redesigned cowling, and it was fitted with a three-blade propeller. This combination produced a top speed of 263 miles-per-hour which made the XSBA-1 the fastest scout bomber in the world at that time.

The prototype was later modified with a higher canopy as used on production aircraft. The engine was also changed to an XR-1820-22, and a three-blade propeller was fitted. It was subsequently used by the National Advisory Committee on Aeronautics [NACA] which later became the National Air and Space Administration [NASA]. (NNAM)

A right front view shows obvious similarities between the SBN-1 design and Brewster's F2A Buffalo fighter which was developed during the same time period. The cowling, landing gear, horizontal tail, and the wings of the two aircraft were very similar. (NNAM)

While other scout bomber designs of the mid-thirties carried their main weapon under the fuselage, Brewster used an internal weapons bay that was completely covered by doors, thus reducing drag on the airframe. A bomb up to the 500-pound size could be carried. The XSBA-1 originally had a very low canopy and fixed solid center section between the two cockpits. As with the XTBD-1, this was later raised to improve visibility and provide room for a rollover structure to help protect the two crewmen in the event the aircraft flipped over on its back.

The Navy placed a small order for thirty production aircraft on September 29, 1938, but these aircraft were built by the Naval Aircraft Factory rather than by Brewster. As a result, these aircraft were given the designation SBN-1, with the N being the manufacturer's designation for the Naval Aircraft Factory.

The SBN-1s were powered by a Wright R-1820-38 Cyclone engine. They were armed with one fixed .50-caliber machine gun, and one .30-caliber flexible machine gun was mounted in the aft cockpit. The largest bomb the aircraft could carry was a 500-pound weapon.

None of the thirty production SBN-1s ever made it to an operational squadron aboard an aircraft carrier. Interestingly, VT-8, a torpedo squadron, used some of them for training before receiving its TBD-1 Devastators and deploying aboard USS HORNET, CV-8.

The Naval Aircraft Factory built the thirty production versions of the scout bomber under the designation SBN-1. Several served with Torpedo Squadron Eight (VT-8) as trainers before that squadron, which would later be decimated at the Battle of Midway, received its TBD-1 Devastators. This SBN-1 rests in a field after a mishap experienced by one of VT-8's pilots. (NNAM)

DOUGLAS SBD DAUNTLESS

The Douglas SBD Dauntless was a direct development of the Northrop XBT-1 and BT-1. This BT-1 was one of fifty-four produced, and it served with VB-6 aboard USS ENTERPRISE. The design similarities between the BT-1 and the SBD are quite evident. (National Archives)

One of the other early monoplane scout bomber designs developed in the mid-1930s was Northrop's BT-1. The prototype XBT-1 was followed by fifty-four production aircraft which saw limited service aboard YORKTOWN and ENTERPRISE. But the Navy was not pleased with the aircraft's performance and requested further development.

Northrop began work on the BT-2 with a more powerful engine, but shortly thereafter the company became the El Segundo Division of Douglas Aircraft. Accordingly, the Navy changed the

manufacturer's designator from T to D, and added an S to indicate the scout bomber role, thus changing the aircraft's designation from BT-2 to SBD.

A production BT-1 was modified to serve as the prototype for the SBD, and orders were placed for fifty-seven SBD-1s and eighty-seven SBD-2s on April 8, 1939. All SBD-1s were assigned to the Marine Corps, and originally the SBD-2s were intended to be used by Navy squadrons. However, some SBD-2s did eventually wind up in Marine units and were used by VMSB-241 at the

The first version of the Dauntless was the SBD-1, fifty-seven of which were produced. These were assigned to Marine squadrons VMB-1 and VMB-2, which were subsequently re-designated VMSB-132 and VMSB-232 by the end of 1941. The SBD-1s were the only Dauntlesses to be painted in the colorful pre-war scheme and markings. This SBD-1 was photographed while still in the pre-war paint scheme, and it was flown by the squadron commander of VMB-1. The three vertical stripes on the rudder were red, white, and blue from front to rear. (NNAM)

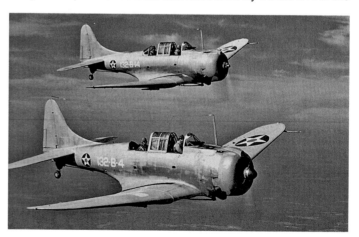

These SBD-1s are painted in the overall gray scheme used during most of 1941. These land-based aircraft belong to VMSB-132, which was the same Marine squadron that had formerly been designated VMB-1. This photograph provides evidence that the larger pneumatic tail wheel was developed for Marine land-based Dauntlesses rather than for the A-24 Banshee as reported elsewhere. This photo was taken in 1941, before any A-24s were ordered. (USMC via Ethell)

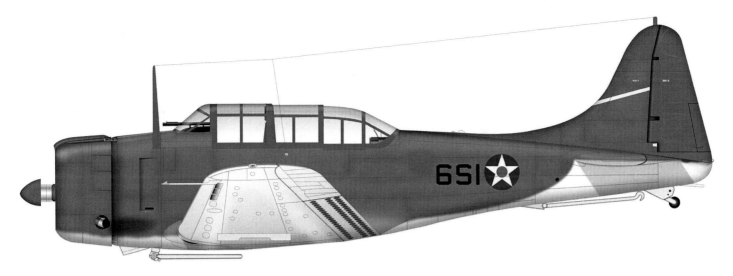

SBD-2 Dauntless, BuNo. 4570, was flown by Lieutenant Clarence E. Dickinson of Scouting Squadron SIX. As Lt. Dickinson flew this aircraft in to Pearl Harbor from USS ENTERPRISE on December 7, 1941, his Dauntless was shot down by a Japanese fighter, but Lt. Dickinson bailed out safely. The radio operator/gunner, RM1c William C. Miller, was killed after firing at and damaging the attacking Japanese plane. Lt. Dickinson made his way to Ford Island and later flew another Dauntless on the afternoon search mission in an attempt to find the Japanese force north of Oahu. At this point in time, Navy aircraft were painted in the Blue-Gray over Light Gray scheme. (Artwork by Rock Roszak)

Battle of Midway.

The SBD-1 was powered by an R-1820-22 engine which provided 1,000-horsepower for take off. Armament included two fixed .50-caliber machine guns in the cowling and a single .30-caliber flexible machine gun in the rear cockpit. Bombs up to the 1,000-pound size could be carried on the centerline station, and weapons up to 325-pounds in size could be carried on each of two underwing racks. This permitted the Dauntless to carry 250-pound standard bombs or 325-pound depth charges for use against submarines.

The SBD-2 was very much the same as the SBD-1, but it did have larger fuel tanks, and two smaller fifteen-gallon tanks were also added inside the wings. This raised the internal fuel capacity to 310 gallons as compared to 210 gallons in the SBD-1. The only external difference between the first two versions was that the carburetor air scoop on top of the cowling was reduced in size on the SBD-2.

The SBD-3 was the first truly combat ready version of the Dauntless. It had increased armor protection and self-sealing fuel tanks that had become absolutely necessary in combat. The R-1820-52 engine replaced the -32 used in the previous SBD-1 and SBD-2. Early production SBD-3s had the same single flexible machine gun in the rear cockpit as found in the SBD-1 and SBD-2, but during the production run of 584 SBD-3s, this was changed to a mount containing two .30-caliber machine guns. Rather than having to load small ammunition boxes on these guns, all ammunition was contained on two belts in one large box. One belt fed each gun, and this meant that the radio operator/gunner no longer

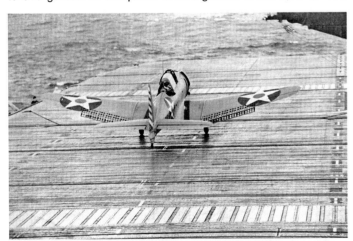

An SBD-3 from VB-6 takes off from USS ENTERPRISE, CV-6, for the raid on Wake Island, in February 1942. At this time, Navy aircraft displayed the national insignia in all four wing positions and both sides of the aft fuselage. They were made as large as possible to avoid confusion with the Japanese red "meatball" insignia, but they still had the red disc in the center of the star. Red and white horizontal stripes were on the rudder. (NNAM)

SBD-3s from Bombing SIX prepare to take off from USS ENTERPRISE, CV-6, in February 1942. During the early months of 1942, the U. S. Navy's aircraft carriers made attacks against Japanese installations on islands in the Pacific, and Dauntlesses played an important role in these raids. (U. S. Navy)

An SBD-3 assigned to VB-8 is respotted on the flight deck of USS HORNET, CV-8, during the Battle of Midway in June 1942. By this time, all red had been ordered removed from the markings on U. S. aircraft. The red disc in the center of the star within the national insignia was painted out, and the red and white stripes on the tail were eliminated. (NNAM)

had to continually reload the weapons with small boxes. Instead, the guns could be fired without reloading until all ammunition was expended.

SBD-2s and SBD-3s were used in the early carrier raids of the war, but by the time the Battle of the Coral Sea took place in May 1942, almost all carrier-based Dauntlesses were SBD-3s. Very few, if any, SBD-2s were still on the carriers during the Battle of Midway the following month as the Navy tried to use only the aircraft with the armor protection and self-sealing fuel tanks. However, nineteen SBD-2s were flown by VMSB-241 from Midway Island during the battle.

At Coral Sea, Dauntlesses were instrumental in sinking the light carrier SHOHO, and heavily damaging the large carrier SHOKAKU. So nimble was the Dauntless, it was often used in the combat air patrol to protect the American carriers. Using their two .50-caliber fixed guns, SBD pilots were often very successful in attacking Japanese torpedo bombers as they attempted to make their runs on American ships. Radio operator/gunners also did a good job protecting their own aircraft, shooting down a number

of A6M2 Zero fighters during the battles. Throughout the entire war, only forty-three Dauntlesses were lost to enemy fighters, and most of these took place in the first seven months of the war. By comparison, the pilots and gunners in the Dauntlesses are officially credited with the destruction of 138 enemy aircraft in aerial combat.

SBD-3s were the aircraft that sank the Japanese carriers AKAGI, KAGA, SORYU, and HIRYU at the Battle of Midway. On June 4, 1942, Lt. Cdr. Wade McClusky led thirty-two SBD-3s from VB-6 and VS-6 from ENTERPRISE to attack the Japanese carrier force. Once over the target, the Dauntlesses dove on KAGA, quickly turning the ship into a blazing inferno. Seeing this as he waited to dive, Lt. Richard Best realized that KAGA was doomed, and he led his section from VB-6 in a turn to the north to bomb AKAGI. Within minutes, Admiral Nagumo's flagship suffered the same fate as KAGA. AKAGI sank beneath the waves, and the drifting hulk of KAGA was finished off by the submarine NAUTILUS.

Meanwhile, Lt. Cdr. Max Leslie was leading seventeen SBD-3s of Bombing Squadron THREE which had been transferred to YORKTOWN while that carrier was at Pearl Harbor for quick repairs after the Battle of the Coral Sea. Leslie and his pilots dove on SORYU, and quickly delivered fatal wounds to the third Japanese flattop. Cdr. Fuchida, who had led the Japanese attack on Pearl Harbor, and who was on the bridge of AKAGI when the American dive bombers attacked, recalled after the war that at one moment, he could look out as far as he could see at the four aircraft carriers and other ships of the Japanese fleet, and he felt that they had complete mastery of the sea. Attacks by American B-17s, B-26s, PBY's, TBD-1s, SB2U-3s, and other aircraft had all been repelled successfully with minimal damage to the Japanese ships. Yet in a space of only four brief minutes, SBD Dauntless dive bombers completely turned the tide of the battle and the war by destroying three of the four carriers.

Only HIRYU escaped the attacks of June 4, but VB-6 and VS-6 were ready to attack again. With YORKTOWN severely damaged and listing, a dozen of VB-3's SBD-3s had recovered aboard ENTERPRISE, and they joined the preparations to attack the one remaining enemy carrier on June 5. Under the command of LT Earl Gallaher, a strike force of twenty-four SBD-3s from VB-6, VS-6, and VB-3 took off from ENTERPRISE without fighter escort to attack HIRYU. One of these had to return to the carrier

An SBD-3 assigned to USS WASP, CV-7, operates near Guadalcanal in September 1942. Note the twin guns in the rear cockpit. WASP was sunk by a Japanese submarine on September 15 during the Guadalcanal Campaign. (U. S. Navy)

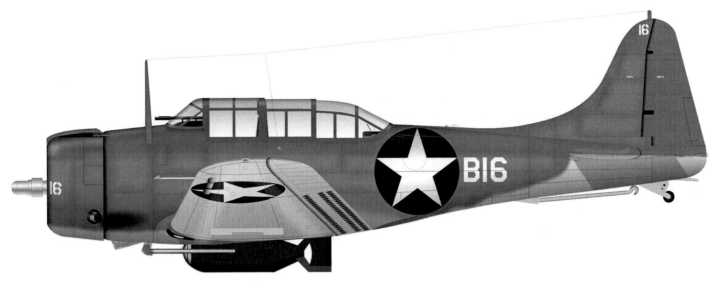

This SBD-4 Dauntless was flown by Lieutenant (jg) Robert Anthony while assigned to Bombing TWELVE (VB-12) flying off USS SARATOGA, CV-3 in the South Pacific in late 1942. The aircraft still sports the Blue-Gray over Light Gray scheme without the red disc in the National Insignia. (Artwork by Rock Roszak)

because of mechanical problems, but the other twenty-three flew on to attack the one remaining Japanese carrier. Thirty minutes later, nine SBD-3s from VS-8 and seven from VB-8 took off from HORNET and followed at some distance behind the aircraft from ENTERPRISE.

The SBD-3s from ENTERPRISE found HIRYU and the pilots of VB-3, VS-6, and VB-6 scored several hits, turning the fourth Japanese carrier into an exploding inferno. By the time HOR-NET's SBD-3s arrived, HIRYU was no longer a target, so they attacked the cruiser TONE but scored no hits.

On June 6, the last day of the battle, six SBD-2s and a like number of SB2U-3s took off from Midway Island to attack the withdrawing cruisers MOGAMI and MIKUMA. Carrier aircraft were launched as well including Dauntlesses and three remaining TBD-1 Devastators. MIKUMA was sunk, and MOGAMI was heavily damaged.

The destruction of the four carriers, all veterans of the attack on Pearl Harbor, along with the loss of their well trained and experienced air crews, marked the turning point of the war in the Pacific and stopped the Japanese expansion to the east. It was a great victory for the U. S. Navy, but the losses were not all on one side. YORKTOWN, damaged by attacks from the air, was finished off

by a Japanese submarine. The destroyer HAMMANN, which was alongside YORKTOWN when the submarine's torpedoes struck the carrier, was also sunk.

The Dauntless gained the nickname "the carrier killer" after these actions, but another name, bestowed on the aircraft by the crews that flew it, became even more popular. Often kidded about how slow the Dauntless was, the crews replied that the SBD in the aircraft's designation stood not only for Scout Bomber, Douglas, they also stood for **S**low **B**ut **D**eadly.

The SBD-4 entered operational squadrons during the second half of 1942. Some participated in Operation Torch as the Allies invaded North Africa. RANGER, CV-4, and the escort carrier SANGAMON, CVE-26, operated SBD-4s during this action. In the Pacific, SBD-4s flew from the light carrier INDEPENDENCE, CVL-22 as well as from several of the fleet carriers.

The SBD-4 differed from the SBD-3 only by having an upgraded electrical system, electrical fuel pumps, and a Hamilton Standard Hydromatic propeller with a bullet-shaped hub that was not covered by a spinner. Most SBD-4s were supplied to the Marines which operated them from island bases.

The most numerous of all Dauntless variants was the SBD-5, 2,965 of which were produced. It had a more powerful R-1820-60

SBD-4s fly over the escort carrier USS SANGAMON, CVE-26, during Operation Torch, the invasion of North Africa. Allied aircraft that participated in this operation, which took place during the last three months of 1942, had a wide yellow border painted around their fuselage insignias. The SBD-4 was essentially the same as the previous SBD-3 except that it had an upgraded 24-volt electrical system and a Hamilton Standard Hydromatic propeller with a rounded hub and no spinner. Some SBD-4s served in Navy squadrons, but most of the 780 SBD-4s were provided to Marine units. (National Archives)

The radio operator/gunner in an SBD-5 from VB-16 has his twin .30-caliber machine guns ready for action as the Dauntless flies over Dublon in 1944. The aircraft is painted in the tri-color camouflage scheme and has the national insignias with the rectangles added. (U. S. Navy)

With its tall hook lowered in preparation for landing, an SBD-5 from VB-10 returns to USS ENTERPRISE after a scouting mission in 1944. Note the Yagi antenna under the wing. (U. S. Navy)

engine which developed 1,200 horsepower. The old telescopic sight was replaced with a reflector type gun sight, and airborne radar sets became standard on this version of the Dauntless. External fuel tanks could be carried in place of bombs on the underwing racks, thus extending the operational range of the aircraft.

The final version was the SBD-6, which had an R-1820-66 engine which produced 1,350 horsepower. Otherwise it was identical to the SBD-5.

Dauntlesses served as the primary dive bomber for the Navy and Marines through 1943. They operated from carriers as well as many land bases throughout the Pacific. In 1944, the Curtiss SB2C Helldiver replaced the Dauntless as the main dive bomber aboard aircraft carriers, but SBD's remained operational from land bases right up until the Japanese surrender.

The USAAF used a few Dauntlesses which it named the A-24 Banshee, but dive bombers never gained widespread acceptance with the Army Air Forces. During the war, the British Fleet Air Arm evaluated nine Dauntlesses, but never put the aircraft into operational service. Number 25 Squadron of the Royal New Zealand Air Force was equipped with Dauntlesses from July 1943 until May 1944 before transitioning to the F4U Corsair. Several Free French squadrons also flew SBDs and A-24s during the war.

The final version of the Dauntless was the SBD-6. It differed from the SBD-5 in that it had a more powerful R-1820-66 engine that developed 1,350 horsepower. This aircraft is painted in the tri-color camouflage scheme which consisted of non-specular Sea Blue on the upper surfaces, non-specular Intermediate Blue on the vertical surfaces, and non-specular Insignia White on the undersides. The addition of rectangles on the sides of the national insignia was ordered on June 29, 1943. (National Archives)

DAUNTLESS COCKPIT & DEFENSIVE ARMAMENT DETAILS

The National Naval Aviation Museum has a beautifully restored SBD-2 that participated in the Battle of Midway. The instrument panel, telescopic sight, throttle quadrant, and slide-out map board are visible in this view. Also note the charging handles for the cowl-mounted machine guns on either side of the instrument panel. (Kinzey)

The large black electrical distribution panel was located forward on the right side of the pilot's cockpit. The large green item is the oxygen canister and regulator. Levers that controlled the landing gear and flaps, the hydraulic hand pump, and the pilot's radio and intercom were also located on the right side of the cockpit. (Kinzey)

The throttle quadrant was located on the left side of the cockpit and below it were the bomb release controls. The black panel had the fuel tank selector valve and the trim control wheels on it. The two red "T" handles activated fire extinguishers. The red lever next to the seat was for the wobble pump. (Kinzey)

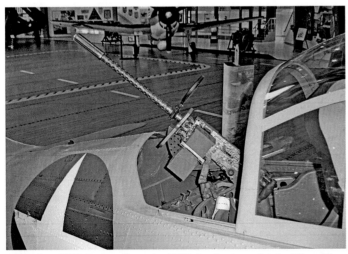

SBD-1s, SBD-2s, and early SBD-3s had a single 30-caliber flexible machine gun in the rear cockpit to provide defense against enemy fighters. Ammunition was fed into the weapon from a small box. Gunners had to constantly change boxes as the small amount of ammunition in each was expended. (Kinzey)

During the SBD-3 production run, twin .30-caliber guns were installed in the rear cockpit. All ammunition was contained in a large box at the rear of the cockpit. A long belt fed the ammunition to each gun. This eliminated the need for the gunner to continually load ammunition boxes for the guns. (Kinzey)

BREWSTER SB2A BUCCANEER

The first production version of the Buccaneer, intended for use by the U. S. Navy, was the SB2A-2, eighty of which were produced. Note the iron ring-and-bead gun sight on top of the forward fuselage. The SB2A-2 did not have folding wings nor an arresting hook, and therefore it could not be operated aboard aircraft carriers. (NNAM)

With its XSBA-1 losing out to both the Vought SB2U Vindicator and Douglas SBD Dauntless in the competition to develop a monoplane scout bomber, Brewster worked on a new design in hopes of acquiring a large production contract from the Navy. Called the Model 340 at Brewster, the Navy ordered a single prototype on April 4, 1939, and designated it the XSB2A-1.

Basically a larger and more powerful development of the XSBA-1, the XSB2A-1 was powered by a Wright R-2600-8 engine that provided 1,700 horsepower, and it made its first flight on June 17, 1941. Top speed was 311 miles-per-hour, and this was impressive for a scout bomber. The design incorporated a power operated turret in the rear cockpit, but a dummy turret was installed in the prototype. This feature did not work out for Brewster as it did for the Grumman TBF Avenger, so production aircraft

had manually operated guns. A bomb up to the 1,000-pound size could be carried in an internal weapons bay. Smaller bombs could be carried on six racks under the wings.

When production began, the initial aircraft were not delivered to the U. S. Navy. The British had ordered 750 Model 340s which it named Bermudas, however only 468 were delivered. Additionally, the Dutch had contracted for 162 aircraft. The British Bermudas began entering service in July 1942, and the U. S. Navy accepted the first of the eighty SB2A-2s it had on order during 1943. In addition to the two .30-caliber machine guns in the rear cockpit, two .50-caliber machine guns were mounted in the cowling and two .30-caliber guns were usually installed in the wings, although provisions were made for four wing guns. The addition of the guns, protective armor, and self-sealing fuel tanks increased the

Sixty SB2A-3s were delivered in 1944, and this was the final production version of the Buccaneer. This variant did have folding wings and an arresting hook, but because they were used exclusively for training from land bases, the arresting hooks were sometimes removed. Although the original design of the Buccaneer featured a power-operated turret for defense against enemy fighters, production aircraft had two flexible .30-caliber machine guns mounted on a ring around the radio operator/gunner's seat like that found in the U. S. Navy's other scout bombers of World War II. (NNAM)

This SB2A-3 has the national insignia adopted in 1943 with the red surround. It is painted in the tri-color camouflage scheme. Note the open bomb bay doors beneath the fuselage. Smaller bombs could be carried under the wings. This photograph also shows the entire cockpit enclosure in the closed position. (NNAM)

empty weight of the SB2A-2 to 9,924 pounds, which was 3,000 pounds heavier than the XSB2A-1 prototype. As a result, top speed dropped to 274 miles-per-hour. Differing from the British, the U. S. Navy chose the name Buccaneer for its aircraft.

SB2A-2s could not be operated from aircraft carriers, because they had neither folding wings nor arresting hooks. These features were added to the sixty SB2A-3s that became the final production variant of the Buccaneer. But the Navy did not really hold the aircraft in very high regard, and all SB2A-3s were used in training squadrons within the United States. As a result, the arresting hooks were often removed.

On March 8, 1943, the Navy took possession of the 162 Dutch aircraft and designated them SB2A-4s. These Buccaneers were essentially the same as SB2A-2s and lacked folding wings and arresting hooks. All were assigned to Marine squadrons for training. Usually all four .30-caliber machine guns were installed.

More than seven hundred Buccaneers and Bermudas were produced for the U. S. Navy and the British respectively before orders were cancelled, but none were ever used in combat by either nation. Brewster produced some Vought Corsairs during the war under the designation F3A-1, but the company never got the large order it needed to survive.

The U. S. Navy took possession of 162 Buccaneers that had been ordered by the Dutch in 1940 for use by the Royal Netherlands Indies Army. These aircraft were designated SB2A-4, but they were not a new or improved version of the aircraft. Instead, they were basically the same as the SB2A-2. This SB2A-4 was assigned to a Marine scout bomber training unit. It has a four-blade propeller, and there is no spinner on the hub. Also note the small bombs carried under the wing. In July 1940, the British ordered 750 similar aircraft which it named Bermudas. (NNAM)

CURTISS SB2C HELLDIVER

The single XSB2C-1 prototype, BuNo. 1758, had a smaller vertical tail than did production Helldivers. It was painted silver, but the upper surfaces of the wings were Gloss Chrome Yellow. The prototype was involved in three crashes, the last of which destroyed the aircraft. (National Archives)

In August 1938, the Navy issued a Request for Proposals for a new scout bomber that would eventually replace the SBD Dauntless. The specifications stated that the aircraft had to be more powerful and carry most of its weapons in an internal bay. It was to have folding wings and be defended by a power operated turret. Six manufacturers submitted designs, but only two were selected for further development. These were the Brewster XSB2A-1 Buccaneer and the Curtiss XSB2C-1. An order for a single prototype of the XSB2C-1 was placed on May 15,1939, and the first flight took place in December 1940. Meanwhile, orders had been placed for 370 production SB2C-1s.

Early flight testing revealed stability problems and poor handling at slow speeds which were critical to carrier operations. The wing area was increased as a corrective measure, but the maximum speed suffered as a result. An engine failure resulted in a crash on February 9, 1941, but the damage was repaired and the aircraft was flying again by May 6. After only ten more flights, the landing gear collapsed causing another delay while the aircraft was repaired.

Flight testing continued to reveal problems, so the airframe underwent considerable modification. The fuselage was lengthened, the bomb bay was enlarged, and more cowl flaps were added to improve engine cooling. The propeller was fitted with cuffs to get more air passing over the cooling vanes of the engine. An oil cooler scoop was added at the base of the cowling, and the

vertical tail was enlarged.

In spite of all these changes, problems persisted, and on December 21, 1941, the wing and tail structures failed in a dive. Although the pilot, Barton T. "Red" Hulse, bailed out safely, the aircraft was destroyed in the resulting crash. Flight tests did not resume for five months when the first production aircraft became available on June 30,1942.

Unlike Grumman, which successfully developed a power operated turret for its TBF Avenger, Curtiss never came up with a suitable turret for the SB2C, which was given the name Helldiver to carry on the tradition of two previous Curtiss carrier-based aircraft. As a result, Helldivers had standard flexible guns in the rear cockpit.

The aircraft was so plagued with problems and poor workmanship that a second production line was set up to make the modifications and add all of the fixes to Helldivers which had already been completed. The USAAF version, known as the A-25A Shrike, was cancelled after only 900 of an order of 3,000 were completed. These included 150 A-25As for the Royal Australian Air Force which disliked the airplane so much that they refused to accept it.

In early 1943, a committee headed by Vice-President Truman issued a scathing report that was severely critical of Curtiss for still not having delivered a single combat-ready Helldiver to the Navy.

The first two hundred production aircraft were divided into Mod

VS-9 and VB-9 were the first squadrons to operate the Helldiver aboard a carrier, when they conducted trials aboard USS ESSEX, CV-9. The results were so bad that ESSEX departed for the war zone with SBD Dauntlesses instead. VB-4 and VB-6 then conducted trials aboard the second carrier to be named YORKTOWN, CV-10. This was the second ESSEX class carrier built by Newport News Shipbuilding in Virginia. The results were so disastrous that the ship's commanding officer, Captain J.J. "Jocko" Clark, stated that the aircraft's only value was as an anchor. YORKTOWN also departed for the war with Dauntlesses in its air group.

Meanwhile, the first of the ESSEX class carriers built by Bethlehem Steel at Quincy, Massachusetts, was commissioned USS LEXINGTON, CV-16, in honor of the first carrier LEXINGTON, CV-2, which was lost during the Battle of the Coral Sea. The new LEXINGTON sailed to the Pacific with SBD Dauntlesses, but the second ship completed at Quincy was USS BUNKER HILL, CV-17. VB-17 conducted carrier trials with SB2C-1, Mod III Helldivers aboard BUNKER HILL, and these were more successful than those previously conducted aboard ESSEX and YORKTOWN. VB-17 departed for the war with their SB2C-1 Mod III Helldivers. The Mod III aircraft reverted back to the twin .30-caliber machine guns in the rear cockpit, and they had a fixed tail wheel with an aerodynamic shroud instead of the retractable tail wheel found on the Mod I and Mod II aircraft.

On November 11, 1943, VB-17 attacked the Japanese during a raid against Rabaul, thus marking the combat debut of the Helldiver. This was the only squadron to fly SB2C-1s in combat. But the war was more than half over by this point, and several more

An SB2C-1 assigned to VB-17 gets a wave off while attempting to land aboard USS BUNKER HILL, CV-17, in 1943. VB-17 was the first squadron to use the Helldiver in combat when it attacked the Japanese at Rabaul on November 11, 1943. (U. S. Navy)

I, Mod II, and Mod III standards as Curtiss tried to solve the problems. Mod II aircraft differed from the original SB2C-1 design by having a single .50-caliber machine gun in the rear cockpit instead of two .30-caliber weapons. The direction finding loop antenna was deleted, and the design of the pitot probe was changed.

The SB2C-1C had two 20-mm cannons mounted in the wings instead of the four .50-caliber machine guns installed in the SB2C-1. This armament would remain standard for all subsequent versions of the Helldiver. This view provides a good look at the aircraft's underside details. (National Archives)

One SB2C-1 was converted to a floatplane by adding two Edo floats. In this configuration, the aircraft was redesignated XSB2C-2. Note the fin added beneath the tail to provide increased directional stability required by the addition of the floats. The larger wheels on the sides of the floats were removable beaching gear rather than being permanently attached. An order for 294 production SB2C-2s was cancelled when the Navy decided it did not need floatplane versions of carrier-based aircraft. (National Archives)

SB2C-3s of VB-20 are launched from the two catapults of the second carrier to be named USS LEXINGTON, CV-16. These are early SB2C-3s as evidenced by the fact that they have the solid dive flaps. Late production SB2C-3s had perforated dive flaps. LEXINGTON originally had SBD Dauntlesses in her air group, but they were later replaced with Helldivers. (NNAM)

months would pass before Helldivers finally became more numerous than Dauntlesses aboard the Navy's aircraft carriers.

The next production version of the Helldiver was the SB2C-1C which had two 20-mm cannons in the wings instead of the four .50-caliber machine guns found in the SB2C-1. This was the first version to see extensive combat action, but two and one-half years of war had passed before the Helldiver finally replaced the Dauntless as the Navy's primary scout bomber. In addition to 778 SB2C-1Cs built by Curtiss, Canadian Car and Foundry produced thirty-eight comparable SBW-1s for the U. S. Navy and twenty-eight SBW-1Bs for the Royal Navy. These were named Helldiver Is by the British, but the aircraft did not meet the approval of the Royal Navy which refused to accept them. Fairchild of Canada built fifty SBF-1s which were also comparable to the SB2C-1C.

The XSB2C-2 floatplane was converted from a single SB2C-1, but this design was never put into production. Instead, the next version to enter service was the SB2C-3 which had an R-2600-20 engine providing 1,900-horsepower for take off. This was 200 more than the R-2800-8 used in the SB2C-1 and -1C. Further, the three-blade propeller, used on previous Helldivers, was replaced by a four-blade propeller which did not have a spinner covering its hub. The extra power was appreciated by the pilots, but the Helldiver was still considered to be seriously underpowered.

Other changes that appeared on the SB2C-3 included a re-

designed canopy for the radio operator/gunner's cockpit, and the structure between the two cockpits was changed. Far more importantly, the solid dive flaps, used on the earlier variants, were replaced by perforated flaps which had a saw-tooth trailing edge. This reduced buffeting during dives, thus improving the Helldiver's accuracy in delivering its bombs. The change to the perforated dive flaps was made during the production run of SB2C-3s, so they were not on the early aircraft of this version. However, they became standard on all subsequent variants of the Helldiver.

A few SB2C-3s were delivered with APS-4 radars, and the antenna was carried in a removable pod beneath the right wing. This replaced the ASB radar with its Yagi antennas. These Helldivers were designated SB2C-3Es.

Curtiss delivered 1,112 SB2C-3s and -3Es, while Canadian Car and Foundry, Ltd., produced 413 comparable SBW-3s. An additional 150 SBF-3s were built by Fairchild of Canada. Helldivers built by the two Canadian companies were usually assigned to training squadrons or to perform patrol duties off the Atlantic coast of the United States.

The SB2C-4, including its SB2C-4E sub-variant, was produced in greater numbers than any other version of the Helldiver, and they could be distinguished from the SB2C-3 and -3E because they had a spinner on their propeller hubs. The remaining two windows on the enclosure between the two cockpits were de-

Two SB2C-4s from VB-6 fly over the fleet late in the war. At that time, VB-6 was embarked aboard USS HANCOCK, CV-19. The aircraft nearest the camera is painted in the overall Gloss Sea Blue scheme which was first directed for use on carrier-based fighters on March 22, 1944. A subsequent directive, issued on October 7, 1944, ordered that the new overall Gloss Sea Blue scheme be applied to all carrier-based aircraft. However, a considerable number of scout bombers and torpedo bombers, already in service when the second directive was issued, finished out the entire war in the tri-color scheme as seen on the SB2C-4 in the background. (NNAM)

An example of the use of tail codes in 1945 is the H on this SB2C-4E assigned to VB-94. Note that the H is painted on the underside of the left wing, and it was also on top of the right wing. The Helldiver is shown flying over its carrier, the second aircraft carrier to be named USS LEXINGTON, CV-16, famously known as the "Blue Ghost." (U. S. Navy)

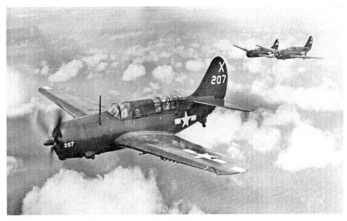

These SB2C-5s from VB-86 were assigned to the second carrier to be named USS WASP, CV-18, in March 1945. They are painted in the overall Gloss Sea Blue scheme, and they have the X tail code assigned to WASP late in the war. (U. S. Navy)

leted, and four zero-length rocket launchers were added beneath the wings to carry 5-inch rockets. Fairly late in the production run, the internal arresting hooks were replaced with external hooks because of corrosion problems experienced with the internal hooks.

Curtiss built 2,045 SB2C-4s and -4Es, while 270 SBW-4Es were produced by Canadian Car & Foundry, Ltd. Fairchild of Canada completed 100 SBF-4Es. Some of these aircraft served in the U. S Navy and the Naval Reserves for several years after the war.

With the large numbers of SB2C-4s entering the Navy, the Helldiver completely replaced the SBD Dauntless aboard the ever-increasing number of ESSEX class fleet carriers as well as ENTERPRISE and SARATOGA. But the large heavy aircraft did not lend itself for use on light carriers of the INDEPENDENCE class nor any of the escort carriers.

Although the Helldiver could carry a heavier load and was faster than the Dauntless, it was not accepted by pilots or maintenance personnel with much affection. It became known as "the big tailed beast" or simply "the beast." More were lost by running out of fuel and crashing into the sea than to enemy fire. The systems were substandard, and failures of these systems often contributed to fatal crashes. At times, the hydraulic system failed, and one or both of the upper dive flaps opened when only the lower flaps were activated for landing. When one of the top flaps opened, the aircraft could roll over on its back and crash before it could be recovered. If both top flaps activated because of a malfunction, the aircraft, already at slow landing speed, would stall and crash into the sea from the low approach altitude.

The final production variant of the Helldiver was the SB2C-5, and it could be distinguished by its frameless sliding canopy

section for the pilot's cockpit. But the internal changes were far more important. With the SB2C-5, the Navy finally believed that Curtiss had corrected most of the Helldiver's problems and had brought the quality of the aircraft's systems up to acceptable standards. Unfortunately, relatively few SB2C-5s made it to operational squadrons before the war ended.

The bomb bay was lengthened, and the cockpit layout was much improved. It had side consoles and the controls and equipment were arranged in a more organized and logical configuration that was on a par with the standards in other military aircraft of that time period. All SB2C-5s were equipped with the APS-4 radar, so there was no need to use the "E" suffix to differentiate them from other aircraft of the same version without that radar system. Another important improvement was that a more reliable fuel system was installed in the SB2C-5.

Curtiss built 970 SB2C-5s, but orders for 2,500 more were cancelled when the war ended. Additionally, Canadian Car & Foundry, Ltd. produced eighty-five comparable SBW-5s. Fairchild of Canada did not produce this version.

In spite of its numerous problems and shortcomings, the Helldiver provided valuable service throughout the final twenty months of the war. Its bombs helped sink Japanese ships, and they pounded targets on the ground.

Throughout its operational life, the Helldiver remained underpowered, and the XSB2C-6 was an attempt to solve this problem. Wright developed the R-2600-22 engine which produced 2,100 horsepower for take off, and this was an increase of 200 horsepower over the R-2600-20. Two XSB2C-6 prototypes were built using existing SB2C-1 airframes, but the project was cancelled when the war ended.

The final version of the Helldiver was to be the SB2C-6. Two XSB2C-6 prototypes were converted from SB2C-1 airframes, but this version was not put into production. These aircraft were fitted with the Wright R-2600-22 powerplant which produced 2,100 horsepower. This was an increase of 200 horsepower over the R-2600-20 used in the SB2C-5. While the more powerful engine offered improved performance, the end of the war, along with a change in doctrine concerning carrier-based aircraft, resulted in the cancellation of the project. (National Archives)

SB2C-5 COCKPIT DETAILS

One of only a handful of surviving Helldivers is on display at the National Naval Aviation Museum. It is an SB2C-5, and details of its cockpit are illustrated on this page. The instrument panel, cockpit floor, rudder pedals, and the control column are visible in this view. The small scope with the rectangular yellow screen in the center of the panel is for the APS-4 radar. (Kinzey)

The pilot's seat and padded headrest are visible in this view. The pilot was protected by armor plating behind and below his seat. The area between the two cockpits was structurally strong enough to protect both crewmen in the event the aircraft flipped over on its back. Almost all of the equipment in this cockpit is original and is well preserved rather than being restored. (Kinzey)

The throttle quadrant, with its propeller and engine controls, was on the left side of the cockpit. The console contained the trim wheels, fuel selector valve, and the bomb release controls. The SB2C-5 was the only version of the Helldiver to have conventional consoles on each side of the cockpit. (Kinzey)

The large circular hand crank for operating the canopy was at the top on the right side of the cockpit. Circuit breakers were on the forward side of the console, while electrical switches, the regulator for the pilot's oxygen supply, and the arresting hook control were on the top of the console. (Kinzey)

GRUMMAN TBF & GENERAL MOTORS TBM AVENGER

Two XTBF-1 prototypes were flight tested by Grumman, and these tests revealed that very few changes were required. As a result, the first production TBF-1s were almost identical to these two aircraft. One of the XTBF-1s is shown here on the ramp at Grumman's plant at Bethpage, New York, during the flight test program. (National Archives)

By early 1940, the United States Navy was certain that a war with Japan was inevitable. Although some older admirals and other planners within the Navy clung to the notion that the battleship was still the center of the fleet, most understood that naval operations in the coming war would be based around aircraft carriers and their embarked air groups. As a result, the Navy issued a considerable number of contracts for new fighters, scout bombers, and torpedo bombers. Among these was a contract issued to Grumman on April 8, 1940, for two prototypes of a new torpedo bomber designated the XTBF-1.

Two weeks after Grumman received this contract, the Navy issued another contract for a competing design from Vought for the XTBU-1. Both aircraft were developed to meet Navy requirements that called for a top speed of at least 300 miles-per-hour, a range of 3,000 miles in the scouting role, and the aircraft had to have an internal weapons bay capable of carrying a torpedo or conventional bombs. Vital areas of the aircraft had to be protected with armor plating, and the fuel tanks had to be self-sealing.

The first XTBF-1 made its maiden flight on August 1, 1941, and the second followed in December. Flight testing revealed that only a few minor changes were needed, so the first production TBF-1s were almost identical to the prototypes.

The aircraft was powered by a Wright R-2600-8 engine that produced 1,700 horsepower for take off. The crew of three consisted of a pilot, a gunner in a power operated turret, and a radio operator who manned a second defensive machine gun in the stinger position. A fourth crewman could be carried in the center cockpit, but this seat was usually unoccupied. A single torpedo or various combinations of conventional bombs could be carried in a long internal weapons bay. The turret had a single .50-caliber

The first production TBF-1s were assigned to Torpedo Squadron Eight (VT-8), but by the time the Avengers were delivered, the squadron had departed for the Pacific in USS HORNET, CV-8, with TBD-1 Devastators. A detachment from VT-8 received six TBF-1s at NAS Norfolk, Virginia, and then flew to the Pacific in an attempt to catch up with the rest of their squadron. This is TBF-1, BuNo. 00380, as it appeared when VT-8 took delivery of it at Norfolk. It still has early 1942 markings, including the red disc at the center of the national insignia and the red and white stripes on the rudder. 8-T-1 is lettered in black on the side of the fuselage. (NNAM)

The same aircraft in the previous photo is shown again here. By the time the six Avengers of VT-8 arrived in the Pacific, it was too late to join the rest of their squadron aboard HORNET. The detachment flew to Midway to enhance the island's defenses. By the time they arrived at Midway, the markings on the TBF-1s had been updated. The size of the national insignias had been increased, and the red disc had been removed. The red and white stripes on the rudder had been painted out. It is shown here immediately after the battle in which it was severely damaged. Miraculously, it limped back to Midway with most of its controls shot out. (NNAM)

Another view of the same aircraft shows the remains of the 8-T-1 resting in the sand of Midway Island. During the battle, this Avenger was flown by Ens. Albert K. (Bert) Earnest. The radio operator was RM3c Harry H. Ferrier, and Sea1c Jay D. Manning was the turret gunner. The other five TBF-1s from VT-8's detachment were all shot down. Manning was killed, and Ferrier was knocked unconscious. Earnest was also wounded. The hydraulic system was shot up, and the aircraft had over seventy holes. The elevator controls were gone, so Earnest had to fly using only his elevator trim tabs. His compass was also destroyed, yet amazingly he flew the severely crippled plane back to Midway Island. (NNAM)

machine gun, and a fixed .30-caliber machine gun was mounted on the top right side of the cowling. Rockets could be carried on launch rails under the wings, but widespread use of rockets did not really begin until the TBF-1C became operational.

Production TBF-1s began to roll off the assembly lines in January 1942, and some of these were rushed to Norfolk, Virginia, for assignment to VT-8. A detachment of pilots and aircrew personnel from VT-8 began an accelerated training program in hopes of quickly joining the rest of their squadron aboard USS HORNET, CV-8, which had departed for the Pacific to carry out the Doolittle/Halsey Raid against Tokyo.

VT-8's detachment departed Norfolk for the west coast, then flew on to Hawaii, but it was too late for them to join the rest of the squadron in HORNET. Instead, the six TBF-1s flew to Midway Island and planned to operate from the island against the approaching Japanese fleet.

On the morning of June 4, 1942, the six TBF-1s were among the planes that took off from Midway to attack Nagumo's carrier force approaching from the northwest. They were led by Lt. Langdon K. Fieberling, flying in 8-T-16, BuNo. 00399. After spotting the Japanese ships, they attacked without coordination with other American planes and without fighter cover. As they made their runs to drop their torpedoes, A6M2 Zero fighters swarmed on them and shot down five of the six Avengers in short order. Only Ens. Albert K. (Bert) Earnest, flying 8-T-1, BuNo 00380, survived, but his airplane was severely crippled. His turret gunner, Sea1c Jay D. Manning, was killed, and the radio operator, RM3c Harry H.

Ferrier, was wounded.

The controls to the elevators were shot out, and Earnest had to fly the plane using only the trim tabs to control pitch. The hydraulic system was also damaged, and this caused the tail wheel to drop down from its retracted position, thus blocking the field of fire for the stinger gun. This left the Avenger completely defenseless, and with his compass destroyed, Earnest relied on nothing short of a miracle to get the crippled aircraft back to Midway. This was very important, because, by getting the Avenger back to the island, Earnest provided the Navy with valuable information about the aircraft's first experience in combat.

Grumman produced 1,525 TBF-1s, but plans had been made to shift production of the Avenger to General Motors' Eastern Aircraft Division. The designation of Avengers produced by Eastern had an M as the letter to designate the manufacturer. The first Avengers built by Eastern were therefore designated TBM-1s. They were essentially identical to the Grumman-built TBF-1, and 550 TBM-1s were delivered. The Royal Navy received 402 TBF-1s and TBM-1s which it originally named the Tarpon Mk I. But the British later adopted the American name and called these aircraft Avenger Mk Is.

A few TBF-1s and TBM-1s were modified for special missions. Several were fitted with special electronic equipment and designated TBF-1Es or TBM-1Es. One was tested for Arctic operations with deicing equipment and was designated TBF-1J. Another was fitted with cameras and became the TBF-1P, and a few TBF-1Ls had searchlights installed in the bomb bay for nighttime illumina-

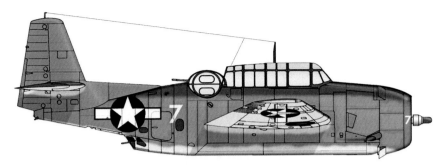

A TBF-1C of VT-24, USS BELLEAU WOOD, CVL-24, as it appeared in June 1944, is illustrated here in the tri-color paint scheme. This aircraft was flown by LT(jg) Ben Tate on June 19, 1944 when he and two other crews attacked and sank the Imperial Japanese Navy aircraft carrier HIYO during the Battle of the Philippine Sea. Tate was awarded the Navy Cross for this action. (Artwork by Rock Roszak)

tion.

Early lessons learned in combat with the Avenger included the fact that the single .30-caliber machine gun in the cowling was not sufficient to suppress enemy anti-aircraft fire as the Avenger carried out its attack. As a result, the TBF-1C and TBM-1C had this weapon deleted. Instead, two .50-caliber machine guns were mounted in the wings, and these proved to be far more effective. Other changes made to the TBF-1C and TBM-1C included moving the antenna mast on top of the cockpit enclosure farther aft, and it was mounted at a vertical angle. The seat in the middle cockpit was removed, and the instrument panel in that cockpit was replaced with a transmitter-receiver for the radio altimeter.

Production of this version of the Avenger included 764 built by Grumman and 2,332 TBM-1Cs delivered by Eastern. The British acquired 334 TBF-1Cs and TBM-1Cs for the Fleet Air Arm, and these were originally named Tarpon Mk IIs. Later, the name was changed to Avenger Mk II.

Several TBM-1Cs were converted to TBM-1CP photographic reconnaissance aircraft, and a few of these did serve on carriers.

In spite of its large size, the Avenger handled beautifully and could be operated easily from the smaller light carriers of the INDEPENDENCE class as well as the several classes of escort carriers. This was very important, because it meant that Avengers could be employed aboard the escort carriers operating in the Atlantic to protect the convoys moving between the United States and Great Britain. They were loaded with 325-pound depth charges in their weapons bays to use against submerged German U-boats. Rockets were carried under the wings to attack U-boats spotted on the surface. The escort carriers (CVEs) usually carried composite air groups composed of Avengers and Wildcat fighters, and eventual-

ly, both types of aircraft were built by Eastern. Similar composite air groups operated aboard the light carriers, but the fighters were usually F6F Hellcats instead of F4F and FM Wildcats in the CVLs.

Although it was designed and classified as a torpedo bomber, the Avenger was armed with standard bombs far more often than it was with torpedoes. The Avenger proved to be a very effective horizontal bomber.

As the Helldiver began to replace the Dauntless in the scouting and bombing squadrons aboard the fleet carriers, the Avenger began performing much of the scouting missions. This was because the Avenger had a better range than the Helldiver, and it was a more reliable aircraft.

One of the technologies that made rapid advances during World War II was radar. Sets soon became small enough to be installed in aircraft for use against targets on the surface and in the air. As the equipment became available, a search radar and associated equipment were added to operational Avengers, including the TBF-1, TBM-1, TBF-1C, and TBM-1C. These aircraft were identifiable by their Yagi antennas under the wings. These looked like small versions of the early television antennas that sprouted from homes across the United States in the 1950s.

The first attempt to develop a true night attack Avenger appeared as the TBF-1D and TBM-1D. Existing airframes were converted to the night attack configuration with the addition of an ASD-1 search radar. The antenna was housed in a pod located on the leading edge of the right wing. These aircraft also retained the ABS radar, but the Yagi antennas were moved to the top of each wing. To lighten the aircraft, all gun armament was removed. These radar equipped TBF-1Ds and TBM-1Ds would be assigned to squadrons and used to direct standard Avengers to targets at

The TBF-1C had significantly more firepower to the front than the TBF-1. The TBF-1 only had a single .30-caliber machine gun on the top right side of the cowling, but this proved woefully inadequate. Beginning with the TBF-1C, all Avengers had two .50-caliber machine guns located in the wings. As he made his attack, the pilot could use these weapons to suppress enemy aircraft fire, and thereby help protect his aircraft. These TBF-1Cs were photographed aboard USS MONTEREY, CVL-26, on December 10, 1943, when the light carrier was participating in the Marshalls/Gilberts Campaign. This picture shows the colors of the tri-color camouflage scheme that was standard for Navy carrier aircraft at that time. (National Archives)

Crewman free the tail hook from the arresting cable on a TBM-1C assigned to VT-20 after the Avenger recovered aboard USS ENTERPRISE, CV-6, on October 10, 1944. (NNAM)

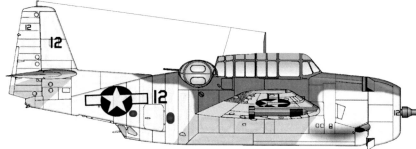

A TBF-1C of VC-69 assigned to USS BOGUE, CVE-9, displays the Atlantic paint scheme of Dark Gull Gray over white. (Artwork by Rock Roszak)

night. The first use of the night attack Avengers was with VC-51 aboard USS SAN JACINTO, CVL-30, in June 1944. Two of the eight Avengers assigned to the light carrier were TBF-1Ds, and this squadron helped develop night attack tactics and doctrine. Three TBF-1Ds were assigned to VT-14 aboard the second carrier to be named USS WASP, CV-18, but the first true night attack squadron was VT(N)-41 which became operational in October 1944 aboard the light carrier USS INDEPENDENCE, CVL-22.

The primary shortcoming of the Avenger remained its lack of power. The R-2600-8 only produced 1,700 horsepower, and fully loaded Avengers struggled into the air as they launched from carriers. Grumman explored the possibility of using the Pratt & Whitney R-2800 which could develop 2,000 horsepower, but all available R-2800s were going into P-47 Thunderbolts, F6F Hellcats, and F4U Corsairs.

Wright developed the more powerful R-2600-10, and this was fitted in TBF-1, BuNo. 00393, which served as the prototype for the XTBF-2. Two other TBF-1s had R-2600-20 engines installed and became XTBF-3s. Both of the new versions of the engine developed 1,900 horsepower, 200 more than the R-2600-8. No

TBM-2s were ordered, but Grumman turned over all production of Avengers to Eastern Aircraft which built 4,664 TBM-3s, making it the most numerous of all Avenger variants. The Royal Navy also acquired TBM-3s and TBM-3Es, and the British called these versions the Avenger Mk III. Sub-variants included the TBM-3P photo-reconnaissance version, a TBM-3J which was outfitted for cold weather operations, the TBM-3L which carried a retractable searchlight, and the TBM-3H which was fitted with a special radar installation.

As with the earlier TBF-1, a night attack version of the TBM-3 was developed and designated the TBM-3D. It carried an ASD-1 search radar antenna in a pod on the right wing. A searchlight was located under the left wing, and as with the earlier night attack Avengers, most or all of the gun armament was removed from these aircraft.

The final production variant of the Avenger was the TBM-3E. Even with the more powerful R-2600-20 engine, the Avenger was still underpowered, so the only alternative was to lighten the aircraft. The .30-caliber stinger gun and its ammunition were removed. The empty weight of the TBM-3E was 300 pounds less

Avengers were used extensively in the Atlantic. Operating from small escort carriers, they provided air cover for convoys moving between the United States and Great Britain. They were armed with rockets to attack U-boats on the surface, and depth charges were carried in the weapons bay to attack submerged German submarines. Navy aircraft which served in the Atlantic were usually painted in a scheme consisting of Dark Gull Gray on the upper surfaces and white on the vertical surfaces and the undersides of the aircraft. This TBF-1C was assigned to Composite Air Group Sixty-Nine (VC-69) aboard USS BOGUE, CVE-9, during May 1944. Note the rockets on launch rails under the wings. A color rendition of another plane from this squadron is shown above. (NNAM)

The first dedicated night attack Avenger was the TBF-1D. These were converted from existing TBF-1 and TBF-1C airframes. The antenna for the ASD-1 search radar was carried in a radome mounted on the leading edge of the right wing. (Grumman)

The TBM-3 had the more powerful Wright R-2600-20 engine which offered an increase of two-hundred horsepower over the R-2600-8 used in earlier Avengers. By the time deliveries of the TBM-3 began, production of the Avenger had been transferred entirely to the Eastern Aircraft Division of General Motors. This left Grumman's production facilities free to concentrate on the F6F Hellcat fighter. This TBM-3 was named "DoT," and it was assigned to Carrier Air Group Forty (CVG-40) aboard the escort carrier USS SUWANEE (CVE-27). A Yagi radar antenna can be seen under the left wing, and a similar antenna is under the right wing. (NNAM)

than the standard TBM-3.

TBM-3Es were equipped with an APS-4 radar, and the antenna for this system was carried in a detachable pod carried beneath the right wing. When not needed, the pod could easily be removed from the aircraft. The scope and other gear associated with the APS-4 were located on the right side of the radio compartment in the aft fuselage.

During the TBM-3E production run, the internal tail hook was replaced with an external arresting hook to reduce corrosion problems.

Throughout the war, the Avenger proved to be one of the most successful and versatile aircraft in service with any nation. Its contributions to victory in the Pacific were significant. For several years after the war, Avengers continued in service with the Navy, and many were modified for special roles. These included both hunter and killer anti-submarine warfare versions, an early warning aircraft, an electronic warfare variant, and a carrier on-board delivery transport.

Several TBM-3s were modified to TBM-3D night attack Avengers. Like the TBF-1D, they had an ASD-1 radar in a radome located on the leading edge of the right wing, and their Yagi antennas were moved to the top of the wings. A high-intensity searchlight was mounted under the left wing. Machine gun armament was usually removed, but the night Avengers could carry rockets on zero-length launchers under the wings. (Eastern)

The TBM-3E was the last production version of the Avenger and was a lightened version of the TBM-3. Most noticeably, the .30-caliber stinger machine gun was deleted from the aft fuselage compartment. An APS-4 search radar was carried in a white pod under the right wing, and its associated scopes were located in the aft compartment. "Satan's Helper" was a TBM-3E assigned to VT-83 aboard USS ESSEX, CV-9, during the closing phases of the war. It was painted in the overall Gloss Sea Blue scheme, and in this photo, it appears to be in new condition. The white geometric "G" symbol markings for ESSEX are painted on both sides of the vertical tail, the upper surface of the right wing, and the underside of the left wing. (NNAM)

The TBM-3E at the National Naval Aviation Museum still has most of its original cockpit in very good condition. Details on the instrument panel are visible in this photograph as are the rudder pedals and the top of the control column. Note the light gray flap control lever in the lower left corner of the instrument panel. Next to it is the longer landing gear control lever, and it has a round knob to indicate the shape of a wheel. The specifically shaped knobs helped insure that the pilot did not move the wrong lever by mistake. The large slot in the center of the instrument panel was for the plotting board that could be pulled out for use. (Kinzey)

Details on the left side of the cockpit were standard for U. S. aircraft of World War II and included the throttle quadrant, trim control wheels, and fuel selector. The pilot's seat had arm rests to help relieve fatigue on flights of long duration. (Kinzey)

The large black box was the electrical distribution panel, and it took up most of the space on the right side of the cockpit. Circuit breakers were on the side of the box, while switches to control the various electrical systems were on top. The smaller black boxes above the electrical distribution panel were controls for various radio equipment. (Kinzey)

The radio operator rode in the aft fuselage compartment, and most of his equipment was located below the turret. Some of the radio gear remains in place inside the TBM-3E at the National Naval Aviation Museum. The radio operator also manned the .30-caliber stinger machine gun in Avengers that had that weapon mounted in the tunnel position. (Kinzey)

ARMAMENT DETAILS

The Avenger's internal weapons bay could carry a single aerial torpedo. The weapons bay was covered by long bi-fold doors on each side. Here a torpedo has been rolled under the aircraft and is ready for loading into the bay. (Kinzey)

Although it was designated a torpedo bomber, the Avenger flew many more missions loaded with conventional bombs than it did with torpedoes. Four 500-pound bombs are loaded into the weapons bay of this Avenger. (Kinzey)

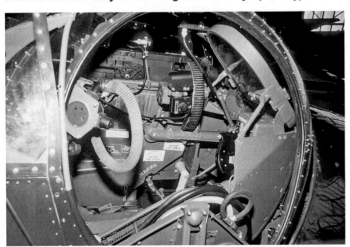

Above: The primary defensive weapon on the Avenger was a .50-caliber machine gun mounted in a power operated turret. This view looks inside the turret and shows the breech of the weapon, the gun sight glass, and the gunner's oxygen hose. (Kinzey)

Right: Avengers, except for the TBM-3E and the specially modified night attack aircraft, had a rearward-firing .30-caliber machine gun mounted in the tunnel position inside the aft fuselage compartment. (Kinzey)

VOUGHT/CONSOLIDATED XTBU-1 & TBY-2 SEA WOLF

The Vought XTBU-1 was a three-place torpedo bomber with a layout much like that of the Grumman Avenger. Notice the defensive machine gun in the tunnel position. (NNAM)

Whenever the Navy wanted a new aircraft developed, it was common practice to solicit proposals from multiple sources within aircraft manufacturing industry. From the submitted proposals, at least two designs would be chosen for continued development, and contracts would be issued for one or two prototypes of each. This was the case when the Navy initiated development of a new torpedo bomber to replace the Douglas TBD-1 Devastator. On

April 22, 1940, just two weeks after giving Grumman the go-ahead to produce two XTBF-1 prototypes of its Avenger, Vought likewise received a contract for a prototype of a very similar torpedo bomber designated the XTBU-1.

Like the XTBF-1, the XTBU-1 was a three-seat aircraft which was defended by a .50-caliber machine gun in a power operated turret and a .30-caliber machine gun in the stinger or tunnel posi-

A right rear quarter view of the XTBU-1 provides a good look at the huge greenhouse canopy with the turret at the aft end. (NNAM)

Consolidated took over production of the new torpedo bomber, and the designation was changed to TBY-2. Although 1,100 TBY-2s were ordered, only 180 were built before the production was cancelled. (NNAM)

tion. A fixed .50-caliber machine gun was mounted in the cowling. A torpedo or conventional bombs could be carried in an internal weapons bay. It was powered by a Pratt & Whitney R-2800-20 engine which developed 2,000 horsepower. The top speed of the aircraft was more than thirty miles-per-hour better than the Avenger, and the Navy placed an order for 1,100 production aircraft in September 1943.

Vought's facilities were already at their limit building F4U Corsairs and other aircraft, so production was assigned to Consolidated at a plant in Allentown, Pennsylvania. The designation was changed to TBY-2 to reflect the change from Vought to Consolidated, and the aircraft was named the Sea Wolf. Production

aircraft could be distinguished from the prototype by the addition of a search radar pod on the right wing. They also had three fixed .50-caliber machine guns instead of just one as installed in the prototype.

The TBY-2 was a very good aircraft which offered excellent performance. However, delays in production caused the Navy to cancel the contract after only 180 were built. This was relatively painless, because the Avenger proved more than able to handle the Navy's requirements for a carrier-based torpedo and horizontal bomber. None of the TBY-2s were ever used in combat. Instead they were assigned to training units in the United States.

The TBY-2 Sea Wolf was powered by a Pratt & Whitney R-2800-20 engine that provided 2,000 horsepower for take off. This was the same powerplant used in the F6F Hellcat, F4U Corsair, and P-47 Thunderbolt fighters. A radome housing a search radar antenna was located on the leading edge of the right wing and provided the aircraft with a night attack capability. Four zero-length launch stubs for 5-inch rockets were under each wing. As with the Avenger, a single torpedo or various types and combinations of bombs could be carried in the internal bay. The Sea Wolf had three .50-caliber fixed machine guns, a single .50-caliber gun in a power operated turret, and a .30-caliber machine gun in the tunnel position. (NNAM)

DOUGLAS XSB2D-1 & BTD-1 DESTROYER

The Douglas XSB2D-1 was originally ordered as a two-seat scout bomber to replace that company's SBD Dauntless. It featured an inverted gull wing, and two power operated turrets were remotely controlled by the radio operator/gunner in the rear cockpit. It also had two fixed 20-mm cannon in the wings. (NNAM)

On June 30, 1941, the Navy issued a letter contract to Douglas for a new scout bomber which was intended to eventually replace the SBD Dauntless. Designated the XSB2D-1, the first of the two prototypes made its initial flight on April 8, 1943. It was a two-seat design with considerable advancements over existing scout bombers then in use or under development. It had an internal bomb bay and was defended by two remotely controlled, power operated turrets. These were operated and fired by the radio operator/gunner in the rear cockpit. Two wing-mounted 20-mm cannon provided firepower to the front.

The aircraft had a tricycle landing gear which was almost unheard of for a carrier-based aircraft during that time period. It was

powered by a large Wright R-3350-14 engine which produced 2,300 horsepower for take off. Top speed was a very respectable 346 miles per hour, which was much faster than the dive and torpedo bombers then in service. The internal bomb bay could carry almost twice the load of the Curtiss SB2C Helldiver.

After the two prototypes were completed and flying, the Navy changed its philosophy about carrier-based aircraft. It decided to develop a new design that would combine the roles and capabilities of both dive bombers and torpedo bombers in a single aircraft. This would mean that more fighters and fewer bombers could be assigned to a carrier's air group without degrading its capabilities. Further, the new type would be a single-seat design without any

A side view of the XSB2D-1 shows the aircraft's stance on its tricycle landing gear as well as the upper and lower remotely controlled turrets. Note how the large fillet of the vertical tail was chopped off vertically to provide clearance for the upper turret's gun. (NNAM)

After the aircraft was redesigned and rebuilt to the single-seat BTD Destroyer configuration, it featured a four-blade propeller without a spinner on its hub. The weapons bay was lengthened, and a large extended fillet was added to the vertical tail. When first flown in the BTD-1 configuration, the aircraft remained painted in the tri-color camouflage scheme. (NNAM)

defensive machine guns which had previously been operated by the radio operator in the aft cockpit. Instead, the bomber would depend on its speed, agility, and the increased number of fighters for defense against enemy aircraft.

As a result of this change in philosophy, Douglas converted the XSB2D-1 to a single-seat design that met the Navy's new requirements. The remotely operated turrets were deleted as was the rear cockpit, but the two 20-mm cannons in the wings were retained. The internal weapons bay was lengthened so that it could carry a torpedo as well as standard bombs, but the engine remained the Pratt & Whitney R-3350-14 used in the original XSB2D-1. Initially it was fitted with a four-blade propeller, and the spinner, used on the three-blade propeller of the XSB2D-1, was deleted. Later, the Destroyer would be tested with the three-blade propeller and the large spinner.

Two prototype XSB2D-2s were tested with a Westinghouse 19B jet engine in the aft fuselage to provide composite power. The air intake for the jet engine was located on top of the fuselage aft of the canopy, however nothing became of this experimental design.

The redesigned aircraft was redesignated the BTD-1 and named the Destroyer. The first flight took place on March 5, 1944. A contract was issued for 358 aircraft, but production was cancelled after only twenty-eight were completed. Some of the twenty-eight BTD-1s were used for various test programs by the Navy and by the National Advisory Committee for Aeronautics (NACA).

Experience gained with the BTD-1 was used by Douglas to develop the XBT2D-1 which was the prototype for what became the highly successful AD Skyraider. This marked the full evolution of the Navy's design and doctrine changes from torpedo and dive bombers to the attack aircraft type that would serve aboard U. S. carriers for many years to come. Eventually, the attack type would be merged with fighter designs in the form of the F/A-18 Hornet and Super Hornet which are in use today.

In its final configuration, the BTD Destroyer had a large three-blade propeller with a spinner, and it was painted in the overall Gloss Sea Blue scheme. (NNAM)

KAISER-FLEETWINGS XBTK-1

The Kaiser-Fleetwings XBTK-1 was one of the single-seat torpedo bombers developed under the new Navy design criteria specifying a single aircraft type to replace both dive and torpedo bombers. Note the external fuel tanks under the wings and the bomb under the fuselage. (National Archives)

The same change in Navy philosophy that caused Douglas to modify the two-seat XSB2D-1 into the single-seat BTD-1 Destroyer also resulted in contracts for single-seat torpedo bombers being issued to Kaiser-Fleetwings, Curtiss, and Martin. Navy requirements specified that the aircraft had to be capable of carrying both a torpedo and conventional bombs, and the crew was to consist only of a pilot. There would be no defensive armament in a second cockpit.

The Kaiser prototype was designated the XBTK-1, and it was ordered on March 31, 1944. The first flight took place in April 1945. Powered by a Pratt & Whitney R-2800-34W with water injection, the aircraft was capable of a top speed of 373 miles-per-hour. Its installation was the first to use exhaust gasses to pump air inside the cowling to cool the engine. The air was then exhausted through slots in the sides of the fuselage. When serving as a dive

bomber, dive brakes were raised from the upper and lower surfaces of the wings rather than being split brakes on the trailing edge of the wings as had been used on earlier designs. Up to 5,000 pounds of bombs or a torpedo could be carried on external racks, and two 20-mm cannons were mounted in the wings

The competing prototype from Curtiss was the XBTC-2, but it did not make its first flight until 1946, well after the end of the war, and it is therefore beyond the scope of this book. However, neither the Kaiser nor the Curtiss design was put into production. Instead, the Douglas XBT2D-1 was developed into the highly successful AD Skyraider attack aircraft, and the Martin XBTM-1 was put into limited production as the AM-1 Mauler. The changes in the designations of these two aircraft from BT for the prototypes to A for the production aircraft indicate the change in design and mission philosophy from torpedo bomber to attack aircraft.

The "picket fence" dive brakes are seen here in the extended position in this rear quarter view. They were hinged at the aft end and folded down flush with the surface of the wings when not in use. (National Archives)

THEATER MAPS

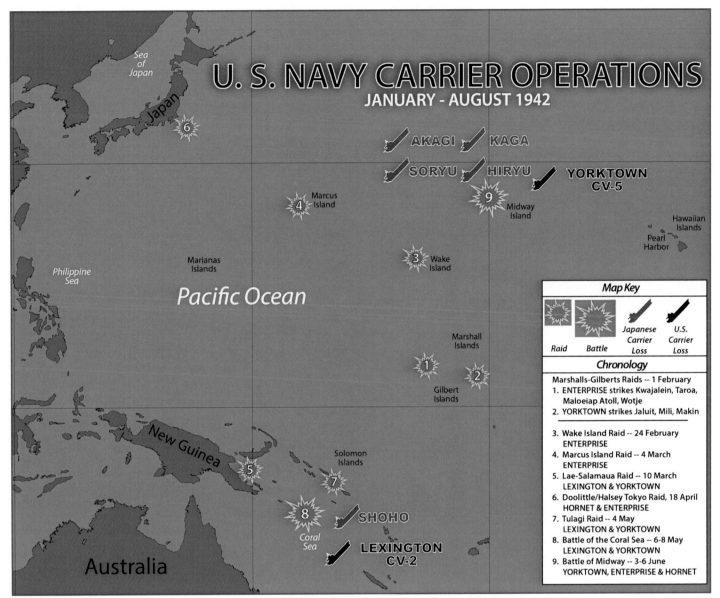

U. S. NAVY CARRIER OPERATIONS
JANUARY - AUGUST 1942

Map Key

Raid	Battle	Japanese Carrier Loss	U.S. Carrier Loss

Chronology

Marshalls-Gilberts Raids -- 1 February
1. ENTERPRISE strikes Kwajalein, Taroa, Maloeiap Atoll, Wotje
2. YORKTOWN strikes Jaluit, Mili, Makin

3. Wake Island Raid -- 24 February
   ENTERPRISE
4. Marcus Island Raid -- 4 March
   ENTERPRISE
5. Lae-Salamaua Raid -- 10 March
   LEXINGTON & YORKTOWN
6. Doolittle/Halsey Tokyo Raid, 18 April
   HORNET & ENTERPRISE
7. Tulagi Raid -- 4 May
   LEXINGTON & YORKTOWN
8. Battle of the Coral Sea -- 6-8 May
   LEXINGTON & YORKTOWN
9. Battle of Midway -- 3-6 June
   YORKTOWN, ENTERPRISE & HORNET

The war in the Pacific began with the surprise Japanese attack on the U. S. naval base at Pearl Harbor, Hawaii, on December 7, 1941. It was a devastating attack against the American Pacific fleet, but the primary target of the attack, the American carriers, were at sea on that fateful Sunday morning. Thus the primary striking power of the fleet survived, and while the country reeled after the attack and the loss of several other critical island holdings immediately afterwards, the turning point of the entire Pacific war was only six months in the future. The primary reason for this was that American naval air power remained intact and the Navy leaders responsible for the prosecution of the war immediately went on the offensive in a way that other aspects of American power could not. While American garrisons at Wake Island, in the Marianas and the Philippines were all overrun and Australia and the Pacific lifeline were threatened, the U. S. Navy conducted operations against a wide range of enemy targets in the six months following the start of the war.

These began with a series of carrier raids against Japanese held islands in the early months of 1942 and the Doolittle raid against Japan in April. The first major engagement between the U. S. and Japanese fleets took place in May at the Battle of the Coral Sea. This marked a turning point in the history of naval warfare, because it was the first battle fought entirely with aircraft. The ships of the opposing forces never came in visual contact with one another. The Japanese lost the light carrier SHOHO, and the carrier SHOKAKU, was severely damaged. The U. S. Navy lost USS LEXINGTON, CV-2, and USS YORKTOWN, CV-5, was damaged. Tactically the battle was a draw, but the Americans won the strategic advantage, because the battle prevented the Japanese from invading Port Moresby.

The turning point in the Pacific war came the following month at the Battle of Midway. Fought over a period of four days between June 3 and 6, four Japanese aircraft carriers were sunk, all of which had been in the force that attacked Pearl Harbor. These included AKAGI, KAGA, HIRYU, and SORYU. The U. S. Navy lost the previously wounded USS YORKTOWN, CV-5. As the sun rose on June 7, 1942, exactly six months after the attack on Pearl Harbor, the Imperial Japanese Navy had lost five aircraft carriers

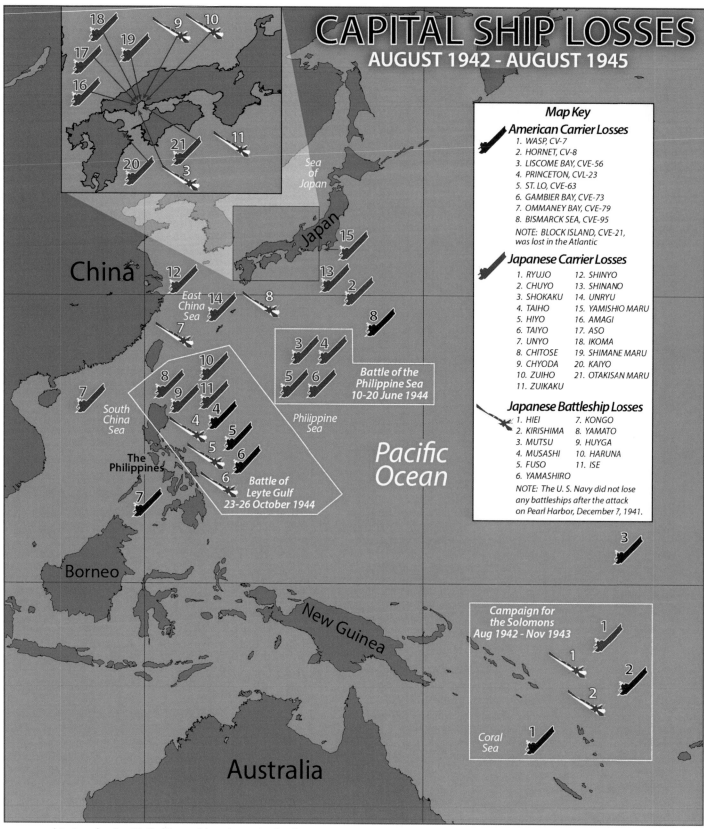

CAPITAL SHIP LOSSES
AUGUST 1942 - AUGUST 1945

Map Key

American Carrier Losses
1. WASP, CV-7
2. HORNET, CV-8
3. LISCOME BAY, CVE-56
4. PRINCETON, CVL-23
5. ST. LO, CVE-63
6. GAMBIER BAY, CVE-73
7. OMMANEY BAY, CVE-79
8. BISMARCK SEA, CVE-95

NOTE: BLOCK ISLAND, CVE-21, was lost in the Atlantic

Japanese Carrier Losses

1. RYUJO	12. SHINYO
2. CHUYO	13. SHINANO
3. SHOKAKU	14. UNRYU
4. TAIHO	15. YAMISHIO MARU
5. HIYO	16. AMAGI
6. TAIYO	17. ASO
7. UNYO	18. IKOMA
8. CHITOSE	19. SHIMANE MARU
9. CHYODA	20. KAIYO
10. ZUIHO	21. OTAKISAN MARU
11. ZUIKAKU	

Japanese Battleship Losses

1. HIEI	7. KONGO
2. KIRISHIMA	8. YAMATO
3. MUTSU	9. HUYGA
4. MUSASHI	10. HARUNA
5. FUSO	11. ISE
6. YAMASHIRO	

NOTE: The U. S. Navy did not lose any battleships after the attack on Pearl Harbor, December 7, 1941.

Battle of the Philippine Sea 10-20 June 1944

Battle of Leyte Gulf 23-26 October 1944

Campaign for the Solomons Aug 1942 - Nov 1943

China

Japan

Sea of Japan

East China Sea

South China Sea

The Philippines

Philippine Sea

Pacific Ocean

Borneo

New Guinea

Coral Sea

Australia

compared to two for the U. S. Navy. More importantly, Japanese expansion and victories were halted, and from then on, the war in the Pacific would be increasingly in favor of the Allies.

The map on this page picks up the time line after the Battle of Midway. It shows both carrier and battleship losses by both sides from August 1942 until the end of the war. What is important to note is that the American battleships ARIZONA and OKLAHOMA, lost at Pearl Harbor on December 7, 1941, were both the first and the last battleships lost by the U. S. Navy during World War II. In fact, they remain the only battleships ever lost by the U. S. Navy. The other battleships that were damaged at Pearl Harbor were repaired, modernized, and placed back in action during the war.

Ten new fast battleships were added to the fleet, and all of these survived the war. But the Japanese lost eleven battleships during the war, and at the time of their surrender, only one battleship, NAGATO, was operational in the IJN.

To a large extent, the war in the Pacific was a carrier war, and the comparison of carrier losses is even more dramatic. A quick glance at the key indicates that the Japanese lost twenty-one aircraft carriers to the U. S. Navy's eight after August 1942. However, these numbers alone do not tell the full story. Of the eight American carrier losses, only two were fleet carriers, these being WASP, CV-7, and HORNET, CV-8. When these are added to the earlier losses of LEXINGTON, CV-2, and YORKTOWN, CV-5, the U. S. Navy's total losses of fleet carriers during World War II was only four. The Japanese lost that many carriers on three separate occasions including at the battles of Midway, Philippine Sea, and Leyte Gulf.

After the loss of HORNET in October 1942, the U. S. Navy did not lose a single fleet carrier for the duration of the war. Of the remaining carrier losses, one, USS PRINCETON CVL-23, was a light carrier, and the other five were all the small, slow, unarmored escort carriers. Considering the scope of the war in the Pacific, it is indeed remarkable and a testimony to the excellent skill of American naval personnel that this record was achieved.

American fleet and light carriers were better built than their Japanese counterparts, but this was only part of the reason behind the success of American carrier operations. Damage and fire control was excellent, and this saved several carriers that were severely damaged. Among these, FRANKLIN, CV-13, and BUNKER HILL, CV-17, received extensive damage that would have destroyed most ships, but the skill of their crews prevented their losses, and both ships sailed back to the United States for repairs under their own power. ENTERPRISE, CV-6, ESSEX, CV-9, INTREPID, CV-11, and LEXINGTON, CV-16, also received Kamikaze and bomb damage, but none were sunk nor even knocked out of the war. Each was repaired and placed back in service to seek a measure of revenge.

Another reason that the U. S. Navy's carriers survived so well was that they were heavily armed with anti-aircraft weapons. The crews of ESSEX class carriers could train over one hundred gun barrels at the attacking enemy aircraft. These included .50-caliber machine guns, 20-mm cannons, 40-mm, and five-inch weapons.

Additionally, the increasing number of fighters aboard the carriers flew effective combat air patrols over the fleet, and screening ships, including fast battleships, heavy, light, and anti-aircraft cruisers, and destroyers could put up a wall of steel and flak that shot down many Japanese aircraft before they ever reached their targets.

The escort carriers did not fare as well, because they did not carry the armor protections that the fleet and light carriers did. They were slower, and they were not large enough to carry extensive anti-aircraft armament. They also did not have as many screening ships as the larger flattops. Yet the loss of only five CVEs by the U. S. Navy in the Pacific remains remarkable considering the large number of these ships that participated in the action.

Of the eleven IJN battleships that were lost, six were sunk by aircraft, three were sunk by gunfire from American surface ships, and one was sunk by a submarine. One, MUTSU, was lost to an accidental explosion while in port.

The five Japanese carriers sunk at the Battles of Coral Sea and Midway were all destroyed by American carrier-based aircraft. Counting those five carrier losses, and the additional twenty-one carrier sinkings shown on the map, seventeen were sunk by American carrier-based aircraft, eight were sunk by U. S. submarines, and one struck a mine. These figures, and the causes of all IJN capital ship losses, clearly illustrate how the aircraft carrier had replaced the battleship as the primary striking force in World War II.

The map also shows how the war continually progressed closer and closer to the Japanese home islands. The sinkings are numbered in chronological order. During late 1942 and throughout 1943, most of the fighting was in and around the Solomon Islands, but by mid-1944, the fighting had moved up further to the northwest and was concentrated near the Philippines. By 1945, the war had reached Japan's doorstep as Okinawa was invaded and American aircraft began to pound Japan itself. IJN losses for that period were along the coastline of Japan or in the harbors and shipyards. In addition to the eleven battleships and twenty-six aircraft carriers, Japan also lost nineteen cruisers, 134 destroyers, 129 submarines, and scores of smaller ships, transports, and auxiliaries during the war.

Carrier-based aircraft from Task Force 38 sank TONE during the bombing of Kure Harbor on July 24, 1945. Their bombs sent the cruiser to the bottom of the shallow harbor with most of her superstructure still above water. TONE is seen here during that attack with bombs falling all around her. (National Archives)

NAVY PAINT SCHEMES
AND MARKINGS

Throughout the history of American naval aviation, the need to identify aircraft assigned to aircraft carriers was recognized, and experiments were conducted using various methods. More often than not, these experiments were carried out at the local level. Being able to identify aircraft for rendezvous purposes was important, especially when more than one carrier was operating in the same vicinity. Throughout the decade of the 1930s, various recognition schemes were directed, many times formalizing practices that had been put into practice in the fleet. By the end of the decade, a comprehensive scheme was in place for carrier-based aircraft which allowed easy identification of the carrier to which any given aircraft was assigned.

By 1937, there were six operational carriers assigned to the fleet, and each carrier was assigned an identification color. The complete empennage of all aircraft assigned to the carrier would be painted in that color. The carriers and their assigned colors were as follows:

USS LEXINGTON, CV-2

USS SARATOGA, CV-3

USS RANGER, CV-4

USS YORKTOWN, CV-5

USS ENTERPRISE, CV-6

USS WASP, CV-7

CARRIER	ASSIGNED COLOR	CARRIER	ASSIGNED COLOR
LEXINGTON, CV-2	Lemon Yellow	YORKTOWN, CV-5	Insignia Red
SARATOGA, CV-3	Insignia White	ENTERPRISE, CV-6	True Blue
RANGER, CV-4	Willow Green	WASP, CV-7	Black

Beyond the carrier-specific tail color, the assigned aircraft carried additional markings to aid with specific in-squadron identification. Most carrier-borne units consisted of eighteen aircraft that were organized into six three-plane sections. The aircraft were numbered sequentially, and each of the three sections had a color assigned. The section colors were standardized as follows:

SECTION 1	SECTION 2	SECTION 3	SECTION 4	SECTION 5	SECTION 6
Insignia Red	White	Insignia Blue	Black	Green	Lemon Yellow

Finally, each section had specified markings, so that every aircraft could be readily identified as a specific aircraft assigned to any carrier, squadron, and section. In addition to the carrier color on the empennage, each aircraft carried a chevron on the upper surface of the wings, and the chevron was in the section color. In the numbering system, aircraft number 1 was assigned to the squadron commander, and he flew at the head of section 1. Aircraft numbers 2 and 3 flew off the squadron commander's wings. The lead aircraft in section 2 carried the number 4, with aircraft 5 and 6 also assigned. Thus, the section leaders were assigned to aircraft numbers 1 (section 1), 4 (section 2), 7 (section 3), 10 (section 4), 13 (section 5), and 16 (section 6). The section leader was identified by having the entire 360 degrees of the aircraft's forward cowling area and a 20-inch wide fuselage band painted in the section color. The number two aircraft in each section had the top half of the forward cowling painted in the section color, while this treatment was given to the bottom half of the forward cowling on the third aircraft in each section.

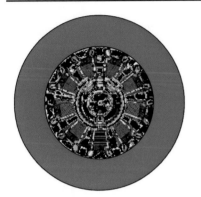

Section 5 Lead
Aircraft #13

Section 5 #2
Aircraft #14

Section 5 #3
Aircraft #15

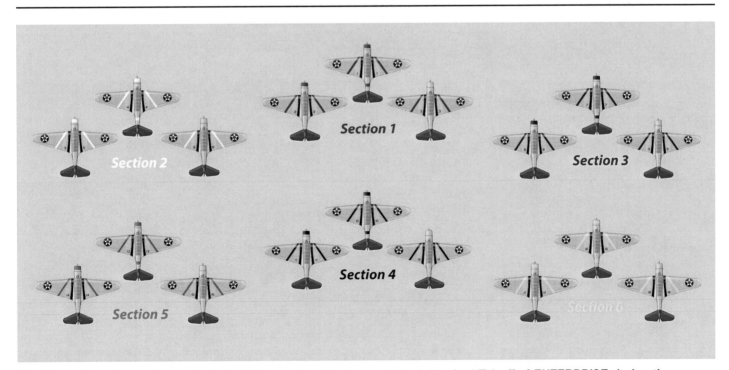

The illustration above shows what a typical squadron fly-by would look like for VT-6 off of ENTERPRISE during the pre-war years. The aircraft are numbered 1-18 and each section could be identified by the color of the wing chevron and cowling markings, with the section leaders also having the twenty-inch fuselage band in the section color. (Artwork by Rock Roszak)

The next carrier added to the fleet was USS HORNET, CV-8, but by the time it was commissioned in October 1941, things had changed completely. With war clouds on the horizon, the colorful pre-war "yellow wings" era came to an end with a directive issued at the end of December 1940 that all ship-based aircraft were to be painted overall Non-specular Light Gray, and in keeping with the need to minimize aircraft visibility, the colorful carrier and section markings were also eliminated. This "gray" period was short-lived, and in October 1941, a directive was issued that canceled all prior instructions and instituted a two-color camouflage scheme as standard. This

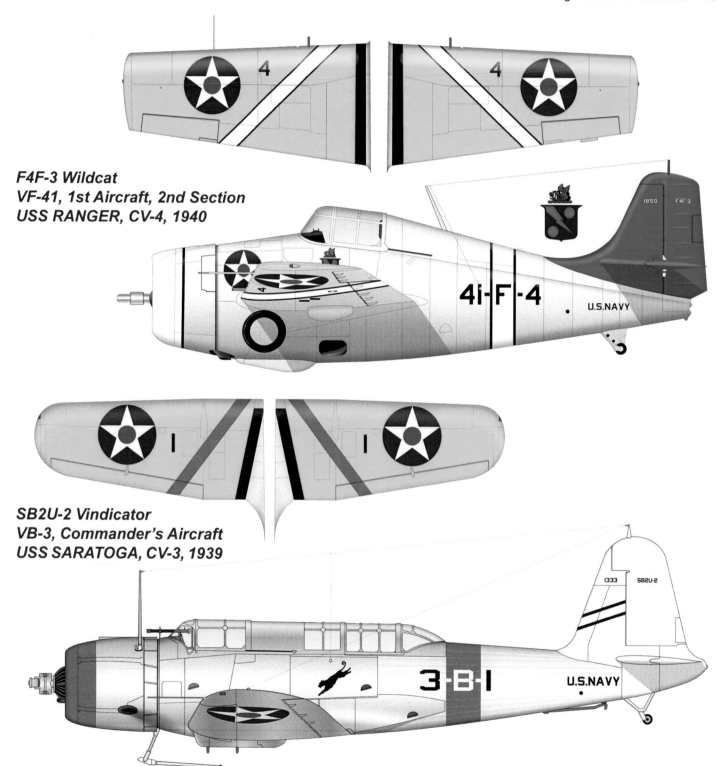

F4F-3 Wildcat
VF-41, 1st Aircraft, 2nd Section
USS RANGER, CV-4, 1940

SB2U-2 Vindicator
VB-3, Commander's Aircraft
USS SARATOGA, CV-3, 1939

The colorful U. S. Navy paint schemes and markings of the 1930s are depicted here. Aircraft were painted with an aluminum lacquer overall, with Chrome Yellow applied to the upper wing surfaces. The intricate unit markings system in place called for colorful tail markings which denoted the carrier to which the aircraft were assigned, while the wing and cowling markings identified specific aircraft within the squadron. Fuselage bands in the section color denoted the lead aircraft for each section. (Artwork by Rock Roszak)

consisted of Non-specular Blue-Gray top and vertical surfaces with Non-specular Light Gray undersides. Camouflage schemes continued to evolve throughout the war, moving from the two-color scheme to a tri-color scheme in February 1943, which actually consisted of four paints made up of three colors: Semigloss Sea Blue, Non-specular Sea Blue, Intermediate Blue, and Non-specular Insignia White. In March 1944, things changed again with a directive that all carrier fighters be painted in overall Gloss Sea Blue, and this scheme was extended to other carrier-based aircraft types in 1945.

SBD-2 Dauntless
VS-5, Commander's Aircraft
USS YORKTOWN, CV-5, 1940

F4F-4 Wildcat
VF-9, Operation Torch
USS RANGER, CV-4, 1942

F4U-1A Corsair
VF-17, Commanding Officer
Lt.Cdr. Tom Blackburn, November 1943

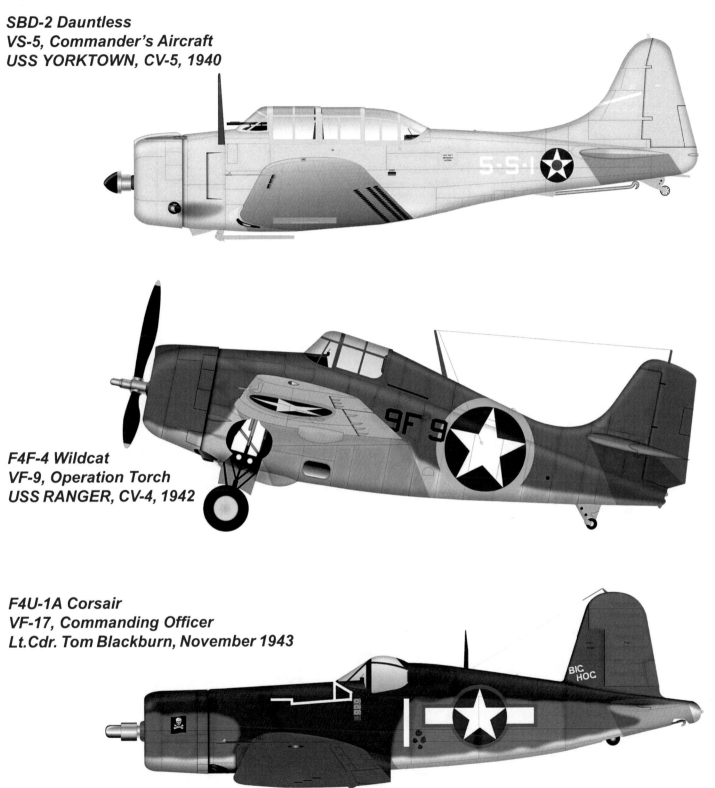

The three profiles on this page illustrate the color schemes seen on U. S. Navy aircraft beginning with the year prior to America's entry into the war through the mid-war years, from the overall Light Gray, the Blue-Gray over Light Gray, to the tri-color scheme.
(Artwork by Rock Roszak)

In the early years of the war, inconsistent carrier-based markings were used, and these were a precursor of what was to come during the final year of the war. Squadron insignias were also inconsistently applied for much of the war, although when present, they were usually under the windscreen on each side of the fuselage. Examples of carrier-specific tail markings dating from 1943 until early 1945 are provided below.

CARRIER TAIL RECOGNITION MARKINGS, 1943-1944

USS ENTERPRISE, CV-6

USS ESSEX, CV-9

USS YORKTOWN, CV-10

USS INTREPID, CV-11

USS HORNET, CV-12

USS TICONDEROGA, CV-14

USS LEXINGTON, CV-16

USS BUNKER HILL, CV-17

USS WASP, CV-18

USS HANCOCK, CV-19

USS INDEPENDENCE, CVL-22

USS COWPENS, CVL-25

USS LANGLEY, CVL-27

USS CABOT, CVL-28

USS SAN JACINTO, CVL-30

Aircraft assigned to escort carriers also needed to be quickly identified, and units aboard these ships also often carried distinctive tail markings. A regimented system would come into being during the summer of 1945. Examples of FM-2s assigned to CVEs prior to that are illustrated below.

USS HOGGATT BAY, CVE-75

USS PETROF BAY, CVE-80

USS RUDYERD BAY, CVE-81

Minsi III, one of the most notable Hellcats of World War II, is illustrated here in its final set of markings. The aircraft was an F6F-5, BuNo. 70143, and it was flown by Commander David McCampbell, the Navy's all-time leading ace with thirty-four confirmed air-to-air victories, while he was the Commanding Officer of Carrier Air Group 15. The aircraft is painted in the overall Gloss Sea Blue scheme, and has the single white stripe across the top of the vertical tail that was applied to all aircraft assigned to USS ESSEX, CV-9, in 1944 prior to the advent of G Markings in January of the following year. Note the printing of CAG on the tail stripe, signifying McCampbell's command status. Minsi III was the last of a series of Hellcats flown by McCampbell during the war, and this profile shows it configured with thirty kill markings, the most it ever displayed in theater. Later, after returning to the United States, he flew a Hellcat with thirty-four kill markings and Minsi III displayed on the side of the cockpit during a publicity tour. (Artwork by Rock Roszak)

Late in the war, the vast expansion of U. S. naval power highlighted the need to institute a regimented carrier recognition markings system for tactical purposes. Gone were the days where carrier raids were carried out by small, two-carrier task groups. The United States entered the war with seven operational aircraft carriers, but by the end of the war almost a hundred fleet, light, and escort carriers were operational, and many task forces included a significant number of aircraft carriers. The requirement to readily determine the carrier to which an aircraft was assigned led to the re-establishment of carrier-specific markings in a series of directives which began in January 1945. A fleet directive issued that month specified a standard set of geometric markings that were assigned to the twenty-seven CV and CVL class carriers assigned to the Pacific Fleet. These became known as "G Markings" for their geometric shapes, and these were applied to both sides of the vertical tails and to the upper right wing. Subsequent directives also called for the markings to be applied to the lower left wing and, in practice, some units applied the wing markings to both wings, top and bottom.

CV/CVL G MARKINGS, JANUARY 1945

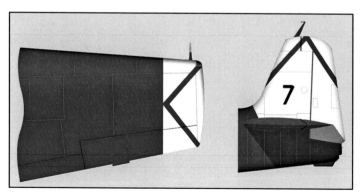

USS SARATOGA, CV-3, AS SPECIFIED

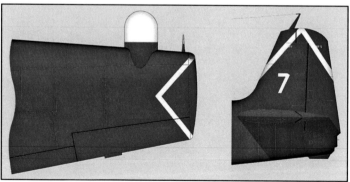

USS SARATOGA, CV-3, AS IMPLEMENTED

CV/CVL G MARKINGS, JANUARY 1945

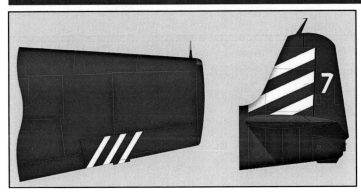

USS ENTERPRISE, CV-6, AS SPECIFIED

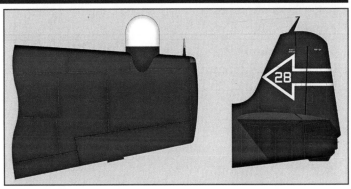

USS ENTERPRISE, CV-6, AS IMPLEMENTED

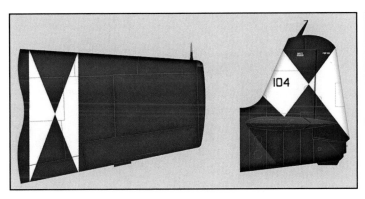

USS ESSEX, CV-9

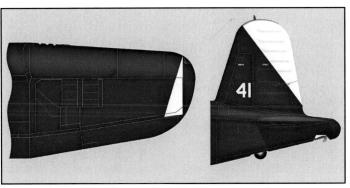

USS YORKTOWN, CV-10

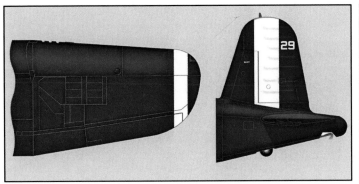

USS INTREPID, CV-11

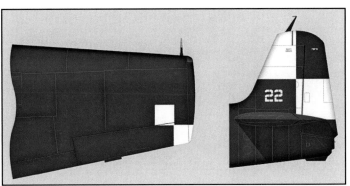

USS HORNET, CV-12

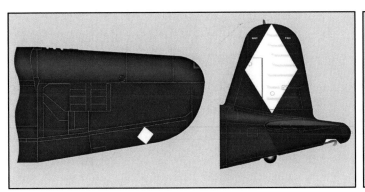

USS FRANKLIN, CV-13

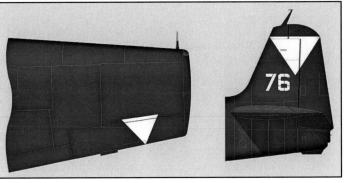

USS TICONDEROGA, CV-14

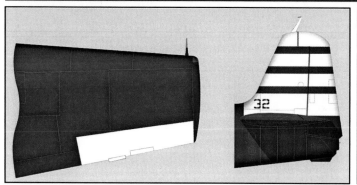

USS RANDOLPH, CV-15

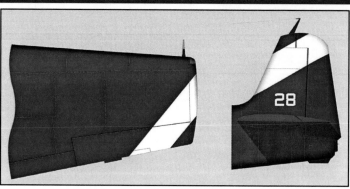

USS LEXINGTON, CV-16

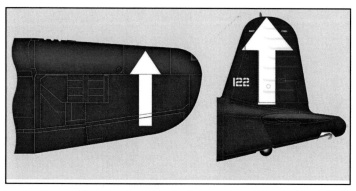

USS BUNKER HILL, CV-17

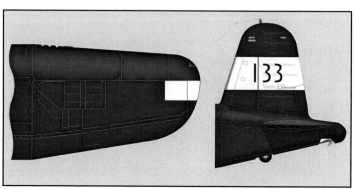

USS WASP, CV-18

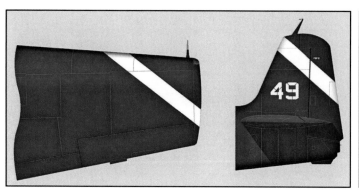

USS HANCOCK, CV-19

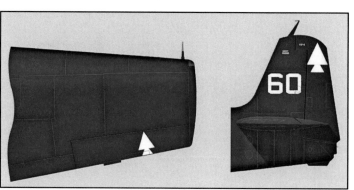

USS BENNINGTON, CV-20

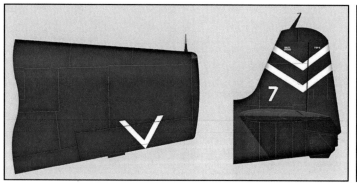

USS BOXER, CV-21

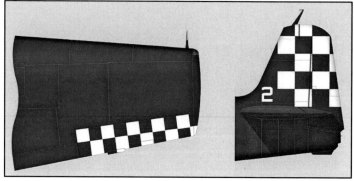

USS INDEPENDENCE, CVL-22

CV/CVL G MARKINGS, JANUARY 1945

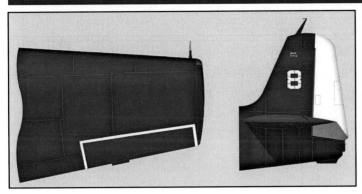

USS BELLEAU WOOD, CVL-24

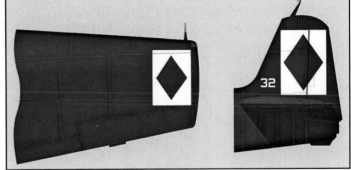

USS COWPENS, CVL-25

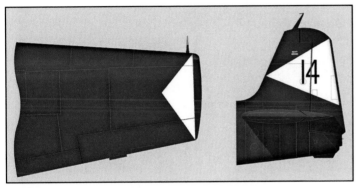

USS MONTEREY, CVL-26

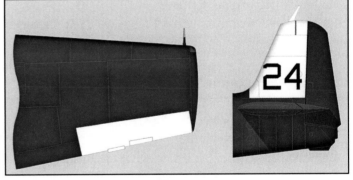

USS LANGLEY, CVL-27

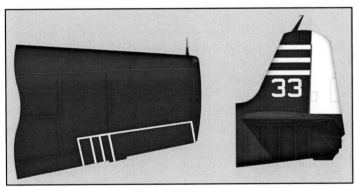

USS CABOT, CVL-28

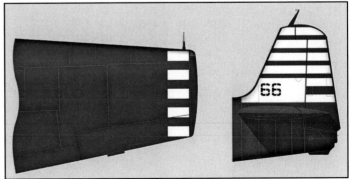

USS BATAAN, CVL-29

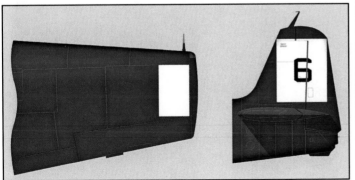

USS SAN JACINTO, CVL-30

USS BON HOMME RICHARD, CV-31

CV/CVL G MARKINGS, JANUARY 1945

USS ANTIETAM, CV-36

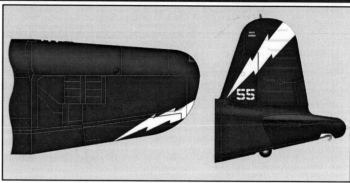

USS SHANGRI-LA, CV-38

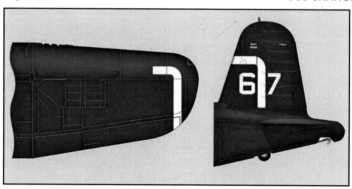

USS LAKE CHAMPLAIN, CV-39

The most numerous aircraft carrier type built during the war were the escort carriers. For those assigned to the Pacific theater, the CVEs were organized into carrier divisions, and a directive issued in June 1945 prescribed a set of markings by division, with standard variations established for up to six CVEs assigned to each division. The standard treatment called for white markings applied to the Sea Blue background on both sides of the vertical tail surfaces and on the upper surface of the right wing. Each division had a major marking design on the tail and upper wing which was carried by all the carriers in the division. Within the division, aircraft aboard the first carrier assigned had a single white stripe on the fuselage/wing and the second carrier had a second white stripe added. The third carrier had a single yellow stripe, while the fourth added a second yellow stripe. The fifth and sixth carriers carried single and double white diagonal stripes, respectively. The following illustrations and listings show the CVE identification markings for the forty-six escort carriers assigned to Carrier Divisions Twenty-Two through Twenty-Nine.

CVE IDENTIFICATION MARKINGS, JUNE 1945

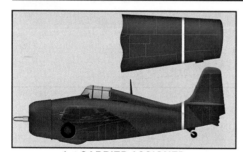

1st CARRIER ASSIGNED

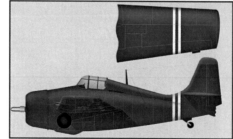

2nd CARRIER ASSIGNED

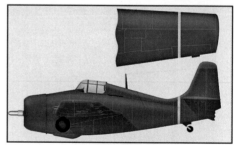

3rd CARRIER ASSIGNED

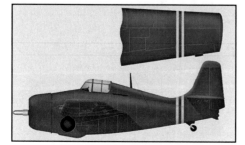

4th CARRIER ASSIGNED

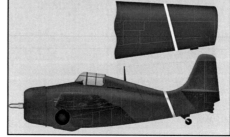

5th CARRIER ASSIGNED

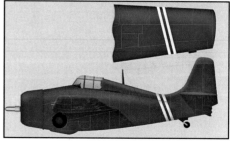

6th CARRIER ASSIGNED

CVE IDENTIFICATION MARKINGS, JUNE 1945

CARRIER DIVISION TWENTY-TWO

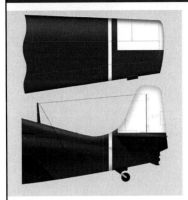

Recognition Marking

White upper vertical stabilizer and forward outer wing areas

Carriers assigned by slot:

#1: USS SANGAMON, CVE-26
   (Illustrated above)
#2: USS SUWANEE, CVE-27
#3: USS CHENANGO, CVE-28
#4: USS SANTEE, CVE-29

Note: Only four CVEs assigned to this division

CARRIER DIVISION TWENTY-THREE

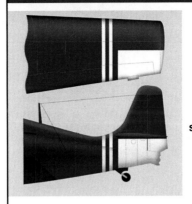

Recognition Marking

White lower vertical stabilizer and aft outer wing areas

Carriers assigned by slot:

#1: USS KITKUN BAY, CVE-71
#2: USS HOGGATT BAY, CVE-75
   (Illustrated above)
#3: USS WAKE ISLAND, CVE-65
#4: USS NEHENTA BAY, CVE-74
#5: USS SHAMROCK BAY, CVE-84
#6: USS ANZIO, CVE-57

CARRIER DIVISION TWENTY-FOUR

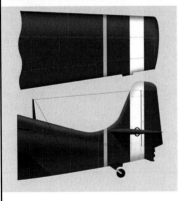

Recognition Marking

White line vertically on vertical stabilizer and chord-wise on outer wing

Carriers assigned by slot:

#1: USS MARCUS ISLAND, CVE-77
#2: USS SHIPLEY BAY, CVE-85
#3: USS SAVO ISLAND, CVE-78
   (Illustrated above)
#4: USS STEAMER BAY, CVE-87
#5: USS CORREGIDOR CVE-58
#6: USS KASAAN BAY, CVE-69

CARRIER DIVISION TWENTY-FIVE

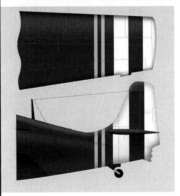

Recognition Marking

Two white vertical lines on fore/aft of vertical stabilizer and chord-wise on outer wing

Carriers assigned by slot:

#1: USS SAGINAW BAY, CVE-82
#2: USS NATOMA BAY, CVE-62
#3: USS PETROF BAY, CVE-80
#4: USS RUDYERD BAY, CVE-81
   (Illustrated above)
#5: USS SARGENT BAY, CVE-83
#6: USS TULAGI, CVE-72

CVE IDENTIFICATION MARKINGS, JUNE 1945

CARRIER DIVISION TWENTY-SIX

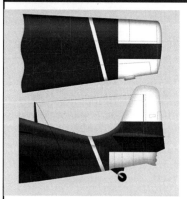

Recognition Marking

white horizontal areas on upper/lower vertical stabilizer and fore/aft on outer wing

Carriers assigned by slot:

#1: USS MAKIN ISLAND, CVE-93
#2: USS FANSHAW BAY, CVE-70
#3: USS MANILA BAY, CVE-61
#4: USS LUNGA POINT, CVE-94
#5: USS SALAMAUA CVE-96
    (Illustrated above)

Note: Only five CVEs assigned to this division

CARRIER DIVISION TWENTY-SEVEN

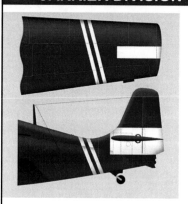

Recognition Marking

White rectangular area at middle of vertical stabilizer and on outer wing perpendicular to chord

Carriers assigned by slot:

#1: USS BLOCK ISLAND, CVE-106
#2: USS GILBERT ISLANDS, CVE-107
#3: USS KULA GULF, CVE-108
#4: USS CAPE GLOUCESTER, CVE-109
#5: USS VELLA GULF, CVE-111
#6: USS SIBONEY, CVE-112
    (Illustrated above)

CARRIER DIVISION TWENTY-EIGHT

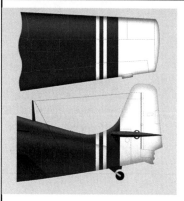

Recognition Marking

White vertical tail and outer wing

Carriers assigned by slot:

#1: USS BENDOVA, CVE-114
#2: USS SALERNO BAY, CVE-110
    (Illustrated above)
#3: USS PUGET SOUND, CVE-113
#4: USS BAIROKO, CVE-115
#5: USS BADOENG STRAIT, CVE-116
#6: USS SAIDOR, CVE-117

CARRIER DIVISION TWENTY-NINE

Recognition Marking

None, though normal striping was applied according to carrier slot

Carriers assigned by slot:

#1: USS SICILY, CVE-118
#2: USS POINT CRUZ, CVE-119
#3: USS MINDORO, CVE-120
#4: USS RABAUL, CVE-121
    (Illustrated above)
#5: USS PALAU, CVE-122
#6: USS TINIAN, CV-123

By July 1945, even the G Markings used by fleet and light carriers had become problematic. Because the G Markings were not always discernible from a distance and were sometimes hard to describe over the radio, a fleet directive was issued that assigned either a one or two-letter code to the aircraft operating on board a specific aircraft carrier. The letters were to be applied in 24-inch high white letters on both sides of the vertical tails and on the upper right and lower left wing surfaces near the tip. Shortly after this system was put into place, the size of the identification letters was increased to 36-inches high, but overall the letter codes proved to be a satisfactory solution. In the 1950s, the single letter tail codes eventually gave way to two-letter codes, and this system is still in use today on the Navy and Marine aircraft assigned to the Navy's various carrier air wings.

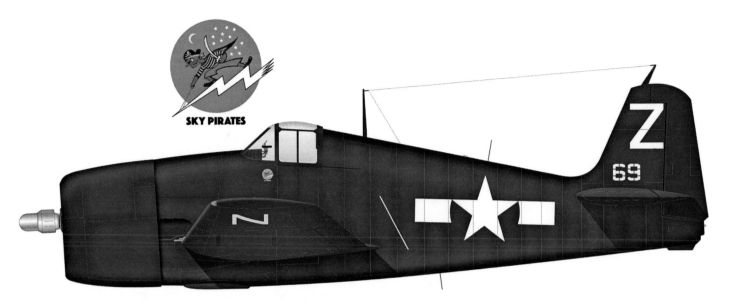

This profile of an F6F-5P from VF-85 aboard USS SHANGRI-LA, CV-38, illustrates the much simpler approach of using letter codes on the tails of aircraft assigned to specific aircraft carriers. The tail code system was instituted in the summer of 1945 and it basically remains the way U. S. Navy aircraft are identified to this day, although two letter codes are the standard. (Artwork by Rock Roszak)

AIRCRAFT CARRIER CODE LETTERS

SHIP	CODE	SHIP	CODE
USS SARATOGA, CV-3	CC	USS RANGER, CV-4	PP
USS ENTERPRISE, CV-6	M	USS ESSEX, CV-9	F
USS YORKTOWN, CV-10	RR	USS INTREPID, CV-11	E
USS HORNET, CV-12	S	USS FRANKLIN, CV-13	LL
USS TICONDEROGA, CV-14	V	USS RANDOLPH, CV-15	L
USS LEXINGTON, CV-16	H	USS BUNKER HILL, CV-17	Y
USS WASP, CV-18	X	USS HANCOCK, CV-19	U
USS BENNINGTON, CV-20	TT	USS BOXER, CV-21	ZZ
USS INDEPENDENCE, CVL-22	D	USS BELLEAU WOOD, CVL-24	P
USS COWPENS, CVL-25	A	USS MONTEREY, CVL-26	C
USS LANGLEY, CVL-27	K	USS CABOT, CVL-28	R
USS BATAAN, CVL-29	T	USS SAN JACINTO, CVL-30	B
USS BON HOMME RICHARD, CV-31	SS	USS ANTIETAM, CV-36	W
USS SHANGRI-LA, CV-38	Z	USS LAKE CHAMPLAIN, CV-39	AA
USS MIDWAY, CVB-41*	YY	USS FRANKLIN D. ROOSEVELT, CVB-42*	FF
USS CORAL SEA, CVB-43*	EE		

Note: The three MIDWAY class carriers were assigned the tail codes indicated, but they did not become operational until after the war.

U. S. NAVY CAMOUFLAGE COLORS -- FEDERAL STANDARD EQUIVALENTS			
COLOR	**FS #**	**COLOR**	**FS #**
Non-specular Light Gray	FS 36440	Non-specular Blue-Gray	FS 35189
Non-specular Sea Blue	FS 35042	Non-specular Intermediate Blue	FS 35164
Non-specular Insignia White	FS 37875	Gloss Sea Blue	FS 15042

EVOLUTION OF THE UNITED STATES AIRCRAFT NATIONAL INSIGNIA

The United States adopted a national insignia for its aircraft with a directive issued in May 1917. It called for a white five-point star inside a blue disc, with a red disc imposed on the center of the design, not quite extending to the inner points of the star. The "American" colors of red, white, and blue, were all represented in the insignia. At various times, the number of insignia on Navy aircraft varied, but when the United States entered World War II, the standard with the Non-specular Blue-Gray over Non-specular Light Gray scheme was four locations: one on each side of the fuselage, one on the top of the left wing, and one on the bottom of the right wing.

Immediately after the United States entered the war, the need for rapid identification caused the Navy to increase the size of the national insignia, increase the number to six on each aircraft (both sides of the fuselage and top and bottom of both wings), and to add thirteen alternating red and white stripes to the rudder. This led to confusion in battle because the red markings were often confused with Japanese aircraft insignia. Accordingly, a May 1942 dispatch directed the removal of the red center from the national insignia and of the striping on the rudder. For the first time, the national insignia did not include all three "American" colors.

In preparation for Operation Torch, the Allied invasion of North Africa, all participating Allied aircraft, including those of the United States Navy, were to have a yellow surround to the national insignia on the two fuselage and two lower wing locations. This was done for air-to-ground recognition purposes, but in practice many participating aircraft also had the yellow surround added to the top wing insignia. In January 1943, another directive reduced the number of national insignia on naval aircraft back to four: one on each side of the fuselage, one on the top left wing, and one on the bottom right wing.

In late June 1943, the United States made the second major change to the national insignia since the beginning of the war. The white star on the blue disc remained, but to this was added a white rectangle on each side, with the entire design having a red border, thus bringing the three "American" colors back into the national insignia.

The final change to the wartime U. S. national insignia was made only six weeks later. Continued concern over confusion with Japanese aircraft resulted in the change to having the border around the entire design changed from red to blue. This would remain the standard until January 1947 when a red stripe was centered on each white rectangle, again resulting in a red, white, and blue national insignia. On aircraft painted in the overall Sea Blue scheme, the Insignia Blue in the insignia was often omitted, but on some aircraft in the Sea Blue scheme, it continued to be used.

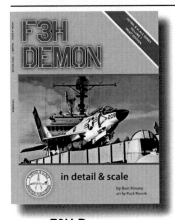

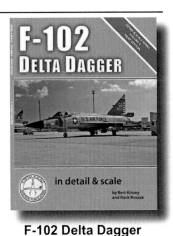

PILOT PAUL THAY
S/C WAT WATKINS

ABOUT THE AUTHOR

Author Bert Kinzey graduated from Virginia Tech in 1968 with a degree in Business Administration. Upon graduation, he was commissioned a second lieutenant in the U. S. Army and was sent to the Army's Air Defense School at Fort Bliss, Texas.

During his eight years as an officer, Bert commanded a Hawk guided missile battery just south of the DMZ in Korea. Later he originated, wrote, and taught classes on the air threat, military air power, and air defense suppression at Fort Bliss.

It was during this time that he did his first writing. Bert was dissatisfied with the existing manuals and other materials available for his classes, because they were inaccurate and incomplete. As a result, he wrote his own reference books and other publications. Although he intended for these to be used only in his classes, they were soon placed on the Army's official publication list and distributed throughout the military.

In 1976, Bert resigned from active duty, but his reputation for being knowledgeable about all aspects of military air power soon led to his taking a civilian position as a subject matter expert on the air threat and world airpower with the Department of Defense. His primary responsibility was to develop a new program to teach the proper identification of both friendly and enemy aircraft, so as to insure the destruction of hostile aircraft and the safety of friendly aircraft. This was the first such program in the world to feature dynamic simulation. Bert has also flown with active, Reserve, and National Guard squadrons on training missions to observe the conduct and procedures of air-to-air and air-to-ground combat. As both an officer and a civilian, Bert often briefed military and political leaders of the United States and other nations on subjects related to air power, the air threat, and air defense.

While he was working for the Department of Defense, Bert started Detail & Scale, a part-time business to produce a new series of books on military aircraft. The Detail & Scale Series of publications was the first to focus on the many details of military aircraft to include cockpits, weapon systems, radars and avionics systems, differences between variants, airframe design, and much more. These books became so successful that Bert resigned from his position with the Department of Defense and began writing and producing books full time. Soon, other well-known aviation writers began writing books for the Detail & Scale Series, so Bert became both an author and an editor. Later Bert added aircraft carriers to the Detail & Scale Series, and he also began a second series called Colors & Markings. Each book in this series focused on a specific aircraft type and illustrated the paint schemes and markings of every unit that had flown that aircraft. Bert also produced a book for McGraw-Hill on the Gulf War entitled "The Fury of Desert Storm: The Air Campaign." In January 2002, Bert produced his one-hundredth aviation publication.

Bert has always taken many of the photographs that appear in his Detail & Scale Series publications, and he believes that whenever possible, it is best that the author take photos in order to precisely illustrate what is being discussed in the text and captions. His has also done photography for other books, magazine articles, websites, and for research and publicity that has been provided to clients. He owns one of the most extensive collections of aviation photographs in the world. Over the years, Bert has given numerous presentations and speeches about military air power, the air threat, military aviation history, and aircraft types, working these into his busy schedule of writing, editing, doing research, taking photographs, and consulting.

In June 2004, health issues caused Bert to retire from his work, and his two series of aviation books came to an end. But in 2011, the Detail & Scale website was created at www.detailandscale.com, and a Detail & Scale Facebook page was also begun. By the end of 2013, Bert had completed the first new title in the Detail & Scale Series in almost ten years, and more books were planned. Initially, these new titles were made available in digital formats, but in 2017, printed versions for titles in the Detail & Scale Series were also added. This new venture was made possible through a partnership with Rock Roszak.

Bert currently lives in Blacksburg, Virginia, with his wife Lynda. They have two children and four grandchildren.

ABOUT THE CO-AUTHOR & ILLUSTRATOR

The co-author and illustrator, Colonel Richard S. "Rock" Roszak, is the son of immigrants who came to America from a war-ravaged Europe. He grew up in Staunton, Virginia, and graduated from Virginia Tech in 1971 as a member of the Virginia Tech Corps of Cadets. He was commissioned into the United States Air Force where he amassed over 2,000 flying hours, mostly in B-52D/F/G and C-135 aircraft, over a 27-year active duty career. His staff tours included time as a special assistant to the Air Force Chief of Staff, liaison officer for strategic aircraft programs to the House and Senate Armed Services Committees, and as the Senior Technical Advisor to the Special Ambassador for assistance agreements to demilitarize strategic nuclear launch vehicles of the former Soviet Union. His final active duty tour was as the Commander, Air Force ROTC Detachment 875 at Virginia Tech, and during his tenure the detachment led the nation in earned scholarships and grew from the 36th to the 8th largest ROTC unit in the country.

After retiring from the Air Force in 1998, Rock spent 14 years on the staff of the Virginia Tech Corps of Cadets, returning to where he began his military career. During those years he established an alumni aviation gallery, which features his artwork of aircraft flown by cadet grads and highlights more than 60 years of military aviation history. An avid modeler in his younger years, he has been a digital artist for more than fifteen years and has illustrated several books in partnership with his friend, Bert Kinzey. In 2017, Rock's role at Detail & Scale expanded when he authored one book and co-authored another. He is also responsible for converting some of the existing digital Detail & Scale Series books to the new print format.

Rock currently lives in Blacksburg, Virginia, with his wife, Patty, two daughters, and six grandchildren.